A Question of Time

Resonate & Blue

First published by Resonate & Blue in 2016
(Imprint of Tatterdemalion Blue)

Words © Carolyn Sparey Fox 2016
Photographs © Carolyn Sparey Fox 2016

Carolyn Sparey Fox has asserted her right
to be identified as the author of this work in accordance
with the Copyright, Design and Patents Act 1988

A CIP catalogue record for this book
is available from the British Library

Cover design and layout by Tatterdemalion Blue

ISBN 978-0-9933114-3-7

Tatterdemalion Blue
8 Upper Bridge Street
Stirling
FK8 1ER

www.tatterdemalionblue.com

A Question of Time

Carolyn Sparey Fox

Carolyn Sparey Fox

Carolyn Sparey Fox was born and brought up in Keswick, in the heart of the English Lake District. With her brother, Jonathan, she was chosen to be a member of the National Youth Orchestra of Great Britain, before being awarded a scholarship to study violin at the Royal Academy of Music in London. Having completed her training she toured North America for two months with the counter-tenor, Alfred Deller, as part of the Deller Consort, after which she settled in London as a freelance viola player, working with most London orchestras and chamber groups, as well as being involved in music for film and backing for pop music. As a member of Yehudi Menuhin's own chamber orchestra she toured Australia, New Zealand and North America, and was also involved in the first London production of *Jesus Christ Superstar*. Carolyn moved to Scotland in the mid-nineteen seventies, taking up the post of principal viola, initially with the Scottish Chamber Orchestra, and latterly with the BBC Scottish Symphony Orchestra. Carolyn has also been commissioned as a composer. This is her second book, the first being, *The Half of it was Never Told*, published by George Ronald. Carolyn is a member of the Baha'i Faith.

Dedicated to my son
Robert Reid Gillies

Contents

Introduction

When my mother passed away on October 21st 2014 at the age of 95, her death marked the end of an era, not only for me personally, but also historically. She had outlived my father by sixteen years, and between them their lives had more or less spanned the 20th century, a century which had seen tremendous transformation and turmoil leading to radical changes in much of Western European society.

At the dawn of the 20th century new inventions, industry, medical breakthroughs and social innovations promised a bright and exciting future with improved living standards for everyone living in Britain; however, with the start of the First World War in 1914 this hope and expectation began to fade as the storm clouds gathered over Western Europe. Millions of people were affected by the war, and many of those who survived were determined to find a way of building a better future for the coming generation. Unfortunately they were unsuccessful, and within a couple of decades, the world was plunged into a second world war.

My father was born before the First World War, and my mother just after it. Thankfully they both recorded their memories, she reluctantly noting down sketchy reminiscences that occasionally left more questions than answers, whilst he recorded almost everything in great detail, including his involvement with the League of Nations Union, his arduous training as a dental surgeon, and his battle with ill health as the Second World War approached.

What follows is a glimpse of life in England beginning in the Edwardian era and ending just after the Second World War. Some family members and friends who accompanied my parents through their early years were a vital part of their story, and are included in the narrative where relevant, as are some locations and addresses which lend a sense of time and place to their story.

Whilst Leslie and Joan Sparey are the subjects of this brief history, they are simply two people plucked from the millions who lived through the same decades, two people who just happen to have been my parents. Their stories are poignant for me personally, but they are also poignant as a reminder of the period during which they lived.

Chapter One

Sparey family roots and early beginnings

The Spareys originated in Wiltshire. My great grandfather, Job Sparey, was born in Codford St Mary in about 1826, just eleven years after the Napoleonic War had ended at the Battle of Waterloo. The Industrial Revolution was still in progress, with the development of machine tools and a growing employment of coal and steam power, laying the foundations for the transformation of society and raising the standard of living, particularly among the middle and upper classes. Not everyone benefitted, however, many being forced to labour for unacceptably long hours in dangerous conditions, with low wages, and without any job security. Indeed, during the Luddite Rebellion between 1811 to 1813, many workers, particularly skilled textile workers, had rioted against what they believed to be an aggressive new class of manufacturers. Just a year later, in 1814, George Stephenson built his first steam engine near Newcastle-on-Tyne, and on September 27th 1825 the Stockton and Darlington railway was opened and inaugurated, with eighteen dignitaries enjoying the journey in a purpose built passenger coach. The world in which Job Sparey found himself seemed rich with possibilities, despite any teething problems which such revolutionary developments brought with them.

Sometime during the 1840s Job left his home in Wiltshire and set out for London, where he began earning his living as a bottle washer, and married a girl named Mary

Anne, from Shoreditch, Middlesex. Victoria had recently become queen, gas lamps were the latest innovation, and with the introduction of the steam train, swathes of housing were being demolished in order to make way for rails and stations; at some point Job and Mary Anne moved to an area of recently built new houses in Dalston, taking up residence in number 1, Middleton Road, Job having changed his occupation to boot maker and, according to the 1861 census, 'employing two men and one boy'. Job and his wife were keen spiritualists, often holding seances in their front parlour; Job was also a strict tee-totaller, and although nothing is known of his involvement in the movement, it's probably safe to guess that his interest came about as a result of the social problems which alcohol undoubtedly caused at the time. Some six children were born over the following years, the oldest, Mary Ann, in around 1856, and the youngest, Herbert, in 1869.

Herbert Sparey was born into a world which to all intents and purposes was full of promise as the 20th century loomed on the horizon. Improvements in equal rights for women seemed imminent in the year Herbert made his appearance, for it was the year during which the Municipal Franchise Act gave single women in the United Kingdom the right to vote in local elections, on condition that, as with their male counterparts, they had lived in a rated property for at least one year. Mahatma Gandhi was born in 1869, the clipper ship, Cutty Sark, was launched in Dumbarton, Scotland, the Suez Canal was opened, and the the first trans-continental railroad was completed in America, connecting the Pacific coast at San Francisco Bay with the existing Eastern U.S. rail network in Iowa, on the Missouri River.

Not much is known of Herbert's childhood years, apart from the fact that at the age of fourteen he left school and was apprenticed to the builder's merchant, Love and Co, not far away from home on the Boleyn Road. Herbert was extremely hardworking, leaving home in the early hours of the morning and returning late during the evening; unfortunately there are no records from this time to give insight to Herbert's relationship with his employer, or what led to him being given the business when his employer retired. Herbert was twenty-one years of age, and this generous gift gave him the opportunity he needed in order to make his life, and that of his future family, comfortable. Just a few years later he was able to give his occupation on his marriage certificate as 'glass and lead merchant'.

Herbert was about 24 when he married. According to family tradition he met Amy Yatman in the Tee To Tum, a club which was specifically for teetotallers. This was most probably the Tee To Tum coffee house at 166, Bethnal Green Road, which had a small theatre attached where performances and talks took place, and where William Morris, poet, novelist, translator, and socialist activist, had addressed meetings in the 1880s. Herbert was a great fan of the well-known actor and monologist, Bransby Williams, and he was thrilled to see him in person at the Tee To Tum theatre.

Although it's not certain, Amy's family most probably hailed from Dorset originally, Yatman being quite a common west country name. Her grandfather, Samuel, was a schoolmaster in the Deptford area of London, where he married Mary Buckland in 1823, and where their son William Samuel was born in 1826. When William Samuel married Elizabeth Crine in November 1862 his occupation was listed on the marriage certificate as 'gas fitter', although Elizabeth later referred to him as a 'master' plumber, most probably due to the fact that he eventually ran a business which employed several workers. According to official records their first child, Walter Alexander, was born in 1862, followed by four daughters, Amy, Jessie, Florrie and Lizzie. Although there is no record of the early years, it's clear that the family were musically inclined, for when the famous Brogden's choir visited Hackney on a prolonged national tour, Florrie and Jessie auditioned, were accepted, and spent the following year on the road travelling throughout Britain. Both girls went on to enjoy successful careers in the Music Hall world, Jessie as a singer and actress, and Florrie as a player of the zither, mandolin and piano. Their sister Lizzie married a man with the intriguing name of Ferguson Nutt Epps, whose uncle, John Epps, had been English tutor to the children of Czar Nicholas II, the last Tzar of Russia, between 1904 and 1908. Despite being the oldest child and only son, Walter Alexander is barely mentioned; 1904 was the last year that his name appeared in the electoral register, living at 11, Gainsborough Square in the Homerton Ward, and it was shortly afterwards that he and his large family emigrated to Canada.

Amy married Herbert Sparey in 1893, when she was about 24, and they spent the first eight years or so of their marriage living over the shop in Boleyn Road. Shortly after their daughter Elsie was born in 1901, they moved to Stamford Hill, a suburb in north London popular at the time with shop-keepers and artisans wishing to escape from the city. Dunsmure Road was a prime location with newly built terraced houses, and number 24, with its six bedrooms, kitchen, scullery, [1] and spacious public rooms leading onto a back garden, promised to be the perfect home for a growing family.

Amy and Herbert Sparey.

Chapter Two

Leslie Sparey, the early years

Leslie Sparey was born on March 8th 1908. Herbert was nearing his fortieth birthday, and already the world greeting his new son was so very different from the one he himself had known as a young boy; aspirin, Coco-Cola and concrete had been invented, as well as the telephone, the zip, the phonograph, the tape recorder and the carpet sweeper, which by 1908 was in competition with the new electric vacuum cleaner. Two Boer wars (1880-81, and 1899-1902) had ended in victory for the British, and Queen Victoria had died after a reign of over sixty-four years, to be succeeded by her son, Edward VII in 1902. The year 1908 brought with it yet more innovations, with the first tentative passenger flight in an airplane travelling all of 600 metres from a field outside Paris, with Henry Ford building the first Model T car in America, and Albert Einstein presenting his quantum theory of light.

During the early years of the 20th century domestic service was still very much a part of British life, particularly in country houses and on large estates. But it was also common at that time for middle-class families to have a resident maid, and the Spareys were no exception, employing a whole series of young women right up to the start of the Second World War. Leslie's earliest recollection was of Ethel Belsher, a very friendly, motherly person to whom he became very attached. Ethel lived in one of the three rooms on the top floor of the family home, and although Leslie didn't have a clear memory of what her daily duties were, apart from serving the meals which were always cooked by Amy, he did stress that all the maids were well-treated, and that they were happy to have work in a good home. Leslie later recorded a few precious memories of his early years in Dunsmure Road; he remembered seeing the Chinese lanterns during local celebrations of the Coronation of George V in 1911, and witnessing the last horse-tram ever to run as it passed the end of Dunsmure Road. He remembered, too, the sinking of the Titanic in 1912, which left a lasting impression on him, as did the untimely death during childbirth of his Aunt Jessie, his mother's favourite sister.

Jessie Yatman, Amy's favourite sister, who died in childbirth.

At about the age of 5, Leslie entered the kinder-garten of Northfield School, a small private school for girls with a couple of classes exclusively for boys. His sister Elsie, now 12, was already well-established in the school, and she no doubt made sure that her young brother was settling in happily during his first few weeks. Leslie didn't remember too much of his early days in school; however, he did remember that on the very first day he managed to make a worm in the clay-modelling class, and that he was so proud of the result that, despite the fact that it wasn't normally allowed, he was given permission to take his worm home with him.

Leslie.

It was at this time that Leslie contracted rheumatic fever, many years before the use of antibiotic drugs. A few weeks later his fever developed into Chorea, or St. Vitus Dance, as it was known, causing uncontrolled jerking of the joints and minor damage to his heart. As a result of his illness Leslie was never able to take part in vigorous sports, and suffered bouts of tachycardia for the rest of his life. Three years later he was quarantined with scarlet fever, isolated in his bedroom with wet sheets draped around the door, a common practice used on the assumption, totally unproven, that scarlet fever could be spread through the air. [2]

Leslie was bored by his isolation, especially since all his toys and books had been burned to avoid contamination, and once the fever had passed he amused himself by dropping his peeling skin over the banisters onto unsuspecting family members below! The family doctor, Thomas Rushbrooke, apparently had a winning way when it came to children, Leslie never forgetting his method of approaching the sick room, "on all fours and growling like a dog!" The days of the group practice were still to come, as was the National Health Service, and Dr. Rushbrooke, who was on call twenty four hours a day, travelled between his patients in a small chauffeur-driven car, cat-napping en route. Many years later he took Leslie to hear the British politician, Isaac Foot, who gave an eloquent and fiery speech on the subject of alcohol, particularly in relation to the brewers' trade which was about to launch an advertising campaign aimed at youth. Leslie remembered well how impressed he was by the power of Foot's oratory, and the effect his words had on the audience.

The family dentist was a Mr Clarkson. Before the Dentist Act of 1921 visits to the dentist could be a risky business since most dentists were unqualified and Licentiates were few and far between. Despite being a qualified dental surgeon Mr Clarkson nevertheless filled the young Leslie with fear. At the time most dentists weren't in the habit of giving injections for fillings, and poor Leslie remembered praying that the electric drill would break down and prevent Mr. Clarkson from drilling, which of course it never did. Unfortunately Mr. Clarkson became an alcoholic, and although it didn't appear to affect the trust of his patients, it certainly unnerved them, as when he neglected to give poor Herbert an injection before a tooth extraction; painful as it was, Herbert later said that it was preferable to having an injection from a drunkard! As if going to the dentist wasn't bad enough, having a haircut was also an occasion of fear and trepidation for Leslie, made even worse when the young barber threatened that if he didn't stop fidgeting he would be turned into sausages, and that there was a machine on hand which would do just that!

Leslie.

There was a rhythm and a routine to life during those days; Sunday was a day of rest and Monday was washing day, Amy and the maid battling with the large copper tub heated over a coal fire, which was also used to heat the flat iron in preparation for the ironing. There was also a weekly ritual of knife cleaning and polishing on a special knife board, since all knives rusted if they were left any longer than a few days. There was general disbelief when Herbert arrived home one day with a stainless steel knife, announcing that the days of cleaning and polishing were a thing of the past, and it was only when he left the knife in water for several hours without any sign of rusting that the household believed him. Another novelty during Leslie's early years was electricity, which only a few privileged people had installed in their homes; on occasional visits to a relative in Leytonstone who had recently had electricity put in, Leslie took great delight in switching the lights on and off, plunging everyone into darkness, and causing much embarrassment to his poor parents! There were several common sights during those early days of the twentieth century, most of which disappeared as new and innovative inventions took their place. One such was the lamplighter, who visited every street at dusk in order to light the gas lamps manually, and another was the muffin man, carrying his wares on a large tray balanced on his head as he swung a hand-bell in order to alert his customers.

Very few people had telephones in their homes when Leslie was a child, and by the time the war broke out in 1914 only a handful out of a hundred or so houses in Dunsmure Road had had one installed. Most people depended on the postal service for communication during those early decades of the century, for it was extremely efficient and reliable, offering deliveries at least five times a day; for instance, a letter posted in central London before 5pm would be delivered by 9.30 the same evening, postage for letters costing a penny or twopence and telegrams about a shilling. During the First World War families whose relatives had been killed at the front were notified by telegram, the sight of the telegraph boy at the front door always bringing a sense of dread and foreboding.

New inventions and ideas were a great novelty, and Leslie well remembered his father taking him to an exhibition at the newly built White City, a vast complex which until it first opened in 1908 with the Franco-British Exhibition and the Summer Olympics, had been arable farmland. The exhibition fascinated the young Leslie, and he particularly remembered the demonstration of a fairly new and innovative gadget known as a vacuum cleaner. According to Leslie's memoir, "it was hand-controlled and needed two people to work it - one moved a handle backwards and forwards which operated the pump and the other moved the suction tube over the carpet".

Music was to become a major love in Leslie's life, and his earliest memories were of musical evenings in the front parlour at home. Herbert played the violin with Elsie accompanying him at the piano, and Amy sang popular contemporary songs such as Roses of Picardy or I Love the Moon, many of them upsetting her young son since they tended to be extremely sad. Herbert also began teaching himself the piano, rising early in the mornings and practising before going off to work. During those early years, it was practically impossible to hear orchestral music anywhere but in the concert hall, for although the concept of radio was in its infancy, the era of radio and television as a means of entertainment was still a long way off. In 1901 Herbert had been one of the first people to own a phonograph, and on recording his voice along with Elsie's as a young child, he was so enthralled by the experience of hearing his own voice for the first time that he was unable to sleep all night! As soon as Leslie was deemed old enough, at the age of 7, to join the music-making, Herbert bought him a violin and began teaching him the basics.

It was at this time that one of Leslie's cousins stayed for an extended period, and since she was to feature much later in Leslie's life, a brief background to her and her family is given here. Ivy was a year older than Leslie, and although their mothers were sisters, their family situations could hardly have been more diverse. It was Ivy's mother, Florrie, who had been accepted to join Brogden's choir as a child, going on to follow a musical career in the music hall which involved a great deal of touring the towns and cities of Britain; it was during one of these tours that she met impersonator and actor, Charles Linden, and although the census for 1901 has them living as husband and wife in a Liverpool boarding house, they weren't officially married until October 1911. At the time of the 1901 census, Charles was 36 and gave his profession as 'music hall artiste facial mime', whilst Florrie, at 26, gave hers as 'music hall instrumentalist'.

Charles Linden was a man with a penchant for collecting professions as well as names, and by 1911 he was calling himself Charles Amandus Carl Linden. Leslie remembered that at one time Charles had decided to set up a society with a view to changing the world, renting an attic room in Oxford Street, central London, in order to give his society a well respected address; despite his enthusiasm and hard work the society only ever attracted two members, and in the end it had to be disbanded. There's no record of exactly when Charles met Mary Florence (Florrie) Yatman, but what is known is that although he was already married, they lived together as husband and wife, producing several children before their official marriage in 1911. They also formed an act which became quite famous on the music hall circuit, with Florrie playing the piano whilst Charles secreted himself behind a screen with a selection of costumes before appearing first as Napoleon, then as Nelson, and a whole series of famous characters of the day. During the 1911 census taken on April 2nd, Charles and Florrie appear as boarders at an establishment in Barry, Glamorganshire (Wales), Charles calling himself Amandus with his occupation as 'music hall artiste', and Florrie noted as his wife of twelve years, but with no occupation other than as mother to their four children, one deceased; Ivy aged 3, and Hugo aged 2 are listed in the census, although nine year old Eva isn't mentioned. There was another daughter, Nora, who doesn't appear in any of the documents, and was most probably born later. The marriage certificate of October 19th 1911 gives Charles' condition as 'widower', and although no mention is made of his first wife's death, it's safe to assume that it was recent, and that it freed Charles to remarry. Daily survival for the Linden family was a constant preoccupation, and married life made no difference to the gruelling schedule. Charles and Florrie were on the road constantly with their children in tow as they moved across Britain, often living in squalid digs and struggling to make ends meet. It's not clear exactly when, or why, but according to Leslie's diary, Eva and Ivy were sent off to Belgium shortly before the war in order to learn French; if he was right, then Ivy could have been no older than five, which is extremely intriguing. Either way, he goes on to say that after six months they were sent home due to the approach of the First World War.

Chapter Three

The Great War 1914 - 1918

The First World War broke out in July 1914, and as the Sparey family holidayed in Eastbourne during the first weeks of August, Leslie was aware of a feeling of foreboding in everyone around him, lifting very briefly when they had the opportunity of watching Ernest Shackleton's ship, the Endurance, as it passed Beachy Head at the start of its long expedition to the Antarctic. Back again in London after the holiday, Leslie was probably too young to really understand the significance of the political situation going on around him, and he settled back into the daily routine of home life.

At that time smog was a regular occurrence in London, covering the city in a blanket of smoke from millions of chimneys and often bringing visibility down to less than a metre; the dense toxic air filled lungs, blackened clothes, and caused people to be lost even close to their homes, Leslie sometimes using the smog as an excuse for being late for school or even not going at all. When air raids threatened during the early days of the war, people took comfort in knowing that they were safe when the smog came down; but smog couldn't be relied on to descend every time there was an air raid, and Herbert decided to turn the coal cellar into an air-raid shelter, furnishing it with a few chairs and using a naked gas flame for light. As soon as the air-raid siren sounded the family made for the cellar, and although they didn't suffer a direct hit, a German Zeppelin was shot down just a few miles away, at Cuffy, Elsie and Leslie watching it come down in flames from their landing window. Leslie's greatest fear was that his father would be called up, especially as the age of compulsory recruitment kept rising, and his constant worry was that the postman would arrive with call-up papers; however, because Herbert ran a builders-supply business he was exempt, since his work was viewed as essential to the war effort. But Leslie was a fearful child, and the war didn't help; he often suffered nightmares, and he was so afraid of the dark that his parents had a door made leading from their bedroom into his. No doubt Leslie's fear intensified when there was an air raid at the school, with the sound of distant bombs, the crackling of anti-aircraft fire, and a few bullets hitting the school itself.

Leslie was 6 years old when war broke out. His memoirs are sketchy regarding personal memories during those difficult years, and although his parents probably did all in their power to shield their children from the trauma of it, there's no doubt that they were aware of enormous changes taking place around them, and of the constant day to day danger.

The Great War, as it became known, brought with it terrors on a scale never before experienced, and which the world hoped never to repeat. The British prime minister, Henry Asquith, declared war on the German Empire on August 4th 1914, and on the 8th the British Government passed the first 'Defence of the Realm Act', allowing it to take over land and buildings which it required for the war effort. The Government also introduced various prohibitions which affected the general public, and these included the feeding of wild animals, loitering under railway bridges, and discussing naval and military matters; further rulings decreed that pubs were to close at 10pm instead of the usual 12.30am, that alcoholic drinks were to be watered down, and that Londoners could no longer whistle for a cab between 10 pm and 7 am; and finally, it was at this point that British Summer Time was introduced. Breaking these rules, and others which came in later, was certainly extremely serious, the maximum penalty following an army court martial being death. During the initial weeks of the war hundreds of thousands of British men voluntarily signed up, numbers only declining after the Somme campaign, which claimed over four hundred thousand British lives alone; it was at that point that compulsory conscription was introduced.

This, then, gives a taste of what Leslie, his family, and the British population were experiencing as the Great War dictated almost all aspects of daily routine and safety. At every level of society people were challenged by the seemingly insurmountably dangerous situation facing them, not least the British monarchy, which until the start of the Great War had been known as the House of Saxe-Coburg and Gotha; it now found itself in a difficult position due to its blood ties to the royal family in Germany, with the current King George V being first cousin of Kaiser Wilhelm II, who acted as Commander in Chief of the German armed forces throughout the war. Thus it was that in July 1917 King George issued an Order of Council in which he changed the name of the Royal family to the House of Windsor, with all descendants of Queen Victoria adopting Windsor as their surname.

One way or another, families living in Britain managed to carry on a semblance of normality as sons, husbands and fathers were away fighting in Europe or further afield. Children still went to school, fathers who weren't away still worked to bring food home, and entertainment was available for those who wished to escape from the difficulties of war for a few hours. It was during the First World War that Charles and Florrie Linden opened the Bijou cinema at Bexhill-on-Sea, where Florrie spent about seven hours a day playing piano for the silent films. Herbert and Amy took the family to Bexhill for the summer holidays several years running, and when Herbert turned up with his violin Charles persuaded him to play along with Florrie, putting up a large notice outside the cinema announcing, 'Orchestra now playing'. Preoccupied by the Lindens' constant lack of funds, Leslie came up with an ingenuous proposition for making money, and was quite sure that in time it would reap rewards; having persuaded cousin Hugo that his scheme would succeed, the two boys planned that they would buy some newly-laid eggs, hatch them, and then by repeating the process ad infinitum eventually end up with a huge chicken factory. Amy was furious when she discovered that the boys had dragged a load of straw up the stairs, and despite Leslie's attempt to explain his plan, she was unmoved.

As previously mentioned, it was at this time that

Leslie's cousin Ivy, Hugo's sister, spent several months living with the Spareys in Dunsmure Road. No reason is given for this decision, or indeed, why Ivy's siblings weren't included in the arrangement. Ivy was a year older than Leslie, and since he had already started to play the violin, he decided to give his cousin some lessons. Little did Leslie realise that he had set in motion events which would eventually determine the life choice not only for Ivy, but for Eva and Hugo as well.

Eva, Hugo and Ivy Linden, Leslie's cousins 1912.

For when Ivy returned home to Bexhill she began teaching her younger brother Hugo, who later became a professional viola player, working in some of London's finest orchestras with some of the best conductors, including Sir Thomas Beecham. Ivy and her sister Eva also became professional musicians, initially performing on a variety of instruments in Ivy Benson's Jazz Band, and several years later becoming entangled in a situation which involved high drama and intrigue, and which will be given due attention when the time comes.

When, early in 1917, German U-boats began sinking Allied supply ships in an attempt to starve Britain and force a surrender, the initial response was to introduce voluntary rationing, which later became compulsory and included bread, meat, sugar and butter. As well as being in danger of attacks from the sea, Britain was faced by the new threat of air raids from German zeppelins and fixed-wing aircraft, with London suffering the first hit during the summer of 1917. This worsening situation combined with Leslie's fragile health following his two serious illnesses persuaded Herbert and Amy to leave London for the countryside nearby, staying initially with friends in Twickenham in order to have a base from which to visit the local estate agents. They eventually found a furnished house in Richmond Road, Staines, a lovely small town on the Thames river, to the west of London; they were joined there by another family, one of Amy's nieces with her husband and two young children, Adrian and Reginald, who stayed with them until the end of the war. [3]

The move out into Staines opened up new vistas for both Leslie and his sister Elsie, for although it was so close to London, Staines was in those days a remote and isolated country town. In London the only access to anything re-sembling countryside had been local parks, but now, with the River Thames only a couple of hundred yards away, they were able to take daily walks along the river bank to Penton Hook Lock, at weekends often walking seven miles or so along the river, past Runnymede, where in 1215 King John signed the Magna Carta, and on to Windsor. There were no buses, and social life was simple and pleasant; Leslie particularly remembered what he referred to as the PSA occasions, PSA standing for Pleasant Sunday Afternoons, in reference to events which were held in the town hall. Although as a young boy he was usually bored on these occasions, there was one event which he found so exciting that the memory of it never left him; this event was the visit of a famous violinist by the name of Leo Strockoff, and not only was Leslie enthralled by his wonderful playing, but he was also extremely excited to hear him practising his violin in the house he was staying in further along the river. Until Leslie was exposed to Strockoff's amazing technique and musicianship, the only violinist he had heard was his father, accompanied by Elsie on the piano, but this exposure to music performance at its highest level was his initiation into a world which was to excite him for the rest of his life.

Leslie didn't attend school when the family was living in Staines, and Elsie took on the job of personal tutor, giving her young brother daily lessons in reading, writing, arithmetic, history and geography. Elsie was only 16 or 17 at the time, but she managed a good disciplined regime, paying special attention to her brother's problem with reading. When her loving perseverance finally paid off, Leslie lost no time in absorbing as much literature as he could, including his weekly comic, The Rainbow, as well as the Children's Newspaper and My Magazine. In another paper he won the prize of a wooden pencil box for writing the best original joke, but unfortunately the paper ceased publishing before his winning entry was printed; if Leslie saw this injustice as a joke in itself he didn't mention it! Although cousin Adrian was seven years younger than Leslie, they enjoyed an almost brotherly closeness, and there were times when Leslie was left in charge of both Adrian and his baby brother, Reginald. Next door to the house was a club for working men, and whilst they were living in Staines the Spareys were considered as caretakers and entrusted with a key; this contact with adults whom he didn't know really helped Leslie to overcome his natural shyness.

The Sparey family, 1922, Leslie, Herbert, Elsie and Amy.

The war dragged on, and by early 1918 it seemed as if the Germans might be winning. Amy's brother, Walter, who had emigrated to Canada, returned to Europe with his two sons in order to join the fighting in France, the younger son, Dick, being shot in the spine and taken to a wartime hospital at Cliveden, the country residence of the Astors. Since it wasn't too far from Staines, Leslie and the family visited him there, and shortly afterwards Dick died as a result of his injuries.

By autumn the tide was turning, and finally, on November 11th 1918 the war was over. Leslie awoke that morning with a sickening headache, as he often did as a child, lying quietly in his room with the curtains drawn. Suddenly, there was great noise and shouting in the street; someone with a telephone had heard that the war had ended, and immediately the news swept like wildfire through the town, Leslie's headache gone and forgotten in a flash. Within weeks the family had relocated to Dunsmure Road, and for a few months life seemed to have returned to normal.

Chapter Four

The post First World War years

The end of the war brought with it hope for a better future; soldiers who had survived returned from a nightmare which many of them were too traumatised to speak of, and as they attempted to adapt to normal life at home, there was general agreement throughout the population that the Great War had been the war to end all wars. But as the disaster of war began to recede, it was replaced by an even worse calamity, for the Spanish flu epidemic of 1918/19 was later viewed as one of the greatest catastrophes of the twentieth century. The first officially reported cases were in Spain, where the King of Spain himself succumbed. In May 1918, Glasgow was the first UK city to be affected, and by June the epidemic had reached London. Those most seriously affected were people between the ages of twenty and thirty, particularly those with strong immune systems; tragically there were young men who had survived the horrendous conditions as soldiers in the trenches, only to return home and perish from flu. By the end of the epidemic it was estimated that up to forty million people had died world-wide, with two hundred and twenty-eight thousand in Britain alone. According to Leslie's memoirs, all the Spareys came down with the flu, but survived, although many of their friends and acquaintances weren't so lucky. No doubt Leslie and Elsie would have heard, or even recited the very apt playground rhyme which children sang at the time:

'I had a little bird,
Its name was Enza.
I opened the window,
And in-flu-enza.'

By the time the war was ending and influenza was raging, Leslie was nearly 10 years old, and had received no regular schooling since leaving Northfield two years earlier. On returning to Stamford Hill he began attending a small preparatory school by the rather grandiose name of Wilson's College, a large Victorian house with a glorified shed being used as an assembly hall and the back garden as a playground. Leslie's memory of the school was that it was "odd in many ways", the teachers seemingly chosen at random, unskilled, badly paid, and most probably young men who had recently been discharged from war service. On one occasion Leslie was left in charge of a class of younger boys who were busy writing an essay on the subject of 'My House'; despite Leslie's appalling spelling, the boys had been told to ask him for help with any spelling difficulties they might have, and when he heard a voice asking him how to spell 'lavatory', he was filled with horror. In a desperate attempt to avoid having to show that he had no idea how to spell lavatory either, his response was simply to announce that since it was a rude word, the questioner shouldn't use it!

In amongst the saved papers and documents is a short poem which Leslie penned at around this period, although whether written as an exercise or in memory of some dear departed family member we will never know. It appears here with Leslie's original spelling:

'When you gave me a bunch of roses
And laid them upon my heart,
you told me in gentle words dear
that the time had come to part.
To this moment I kept those roses
in memery of the day

When you left me alone in this world dear
For the land afar away.
Although they are dead and faded
They are as much to me
As all the roses in the world
Because I cherish thee.'

Despite the drawbacks of Wilson's College, Leslie made two meaningful friendships which were to influence his future, one of them with a young student teacher by the name of Jack Horn who introduced his eager young students to wireless transmission through an experiment he carried out in their presence; as they sat in a circle around a loud-speaker, they were astonished to hear a man's voice and some music, seemingly coming out of nowhere. This was in the year 1920 or thereabouts, several years before the era of broadcasting, and the experience was the catalyst for Leslie's interest in radio, which led a few years later to him making one of the first amateur radio receivers in North London. Leslie's other friendship was with fellow student

Dick Scully, who also lived in Dunsmure Road and who was a phenomenal pianist, even as a young boy. His formidable repertoire of Beethoven, Chopin, and other great piano composers, opened up a new world of music to Leslie. Dick also had a good sense of humour and was a great mimic and leg-puller; on several occasions he successfully disguised himself as a middle-aged woman, singing in a high voice as he accompanied himself at the piano.

It was at around this time that Herbert bought Leslie a bicycle; although there were still relatively few cars on the roads in the 1920s, cyclists nevertheless had to make sure that their wheels didn't run into the tram-lines. Herbert obviously felt that Leslie was capable of taking care when he was cycling, and it became something which he enjoyed more and more as he ventured further afield into the countryside where the space and the freedom gave him the time he needed to think through problems as he sped along the quiet suburban and country roads.

Whilst Wilson's College gave Leslie the beginnings of an education which had been minimal during the war years, he was still behind for his age, something which was soon rectified by two very good private coaches; one of them was a lady who coached him in English, Maths and French, and the other a retired classics teacher who taught him Latin, which soon became one of Leslie's favourite and best subjects. In the meantime Herbert began looking for a good grammar school, eventually securing an interview and entrance exam at Mercers School, in the City of London. The initial interview was conducted by the austere and authoritarian headmaster, Charles Bickell, who had a deep and sonorous voice and who terrified young Leslie so much that when he was suddenly asked, "What is a half plus a third?" his mind went blank, and he nervously blurted out the wrong answer; as Herbert talked with Mr. Bickell, Leslie suddenly remembered the correct answer, timidly venturing, "five sixths". "Too late" Mr. Bickell growled, which poor Leslie felt was extremely unfair. Nevertheless, a written exam was granted, and following a further interview with a Mr. Boon, he was accepted at Mercers.

During his six years as a school-boy at Mercers Leslie travelled the four miles to school and home again by tram, passing along Roseberry Avenue where he was able to see the foundations being laid for the rebuilding of Sadlers Wells theatre; curiously, during the ten-day general strike of May 1926 he walked to school and back several times, offering no explanation as to why he didn't use his bicycle. Mercers school was an independent school operated by the Worshipful Company of Mercers, and had a history going as far back as the 16th century. Leslie's years as a student there gave him a deep and lasting interest in the city of London, its history, traditions and buildings, culminating many decades later in his application and acceptance as a Freeman of the City. However, his initial months at Mercer's weren't plain sailing; his French and maths were of an extremely poor standard, and since he was the oldest boy in his class he felt somewhat inferior to his fellow students. Thankfully his Latin skills were unmatched amongst his peers, which no doubt helped him in regaining a degree of self-esteem, and he also discovered a talent for essay writing, his work often being chosen to be read out in class. French and history were taught by [4] B.C Boulter, who was a writer and illustrator in his own right, and with whom Leslie kept in touch for over thirty years.

Shanklin 1921, Leslie and Elsie, second and third from the left.

Due to his debilitating childhood illnesses Leslie was exempted from all sports, which meant that during the school break times he had to stand quietly in the playground whilst his fellow students "dashed about energetically". Herbert was of the opinion that his son's stamina would improve if he engaged in at least a minimum of physical training, and he arranged for Elsie's fiancé, Wallis Roach, to give him regular running exercises round the garden. Wallis took his task seriously, and Leslie dutifully carried out his instructions, far too nervous to complain of the chest pains he suffered as a result; thankfully the exercise sessions were soon dropped, and it's quite likely that if he had carried on

Leslie's fragile health would have been seriously compromised. A side effect of the acute rheumatism he had suffered a few years earlier was weakness of the ankles, and Leslie's doctor prescribed 'straight' boots which were interchangeable, moving from one foot to the other every other day; it's not exactly clear how these boots were made, how they fitted both feet, or what they were supposed to achieve, and Leslie only referred to them briefly in his memoirs.

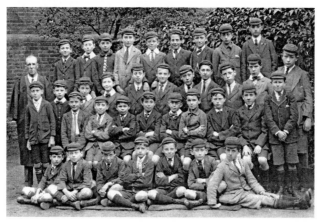

Wilson's College, Leslie, second row up, third from the right.

The Spareys weren't a religious family, the only contact Leslie having with anything of a Christian nature during his early years being the Lord's Prayer, which was taught to him by his mother. Christmas was a secular celebration, and Leslie recalled that the whole family were slightly puzzled when friends sent them cards with a Christian message. Leslie was first exposed to the reality of the Christian religion as a student at Mercers, experiencing the Bible and the Creed first hand, and learning about Christian concepts and laws; the matter of circumcision obviously preoccupied all the boys in Leslie's class, and when they embarrassed their teacher, Mr. Boon, by asking him to explain it to them, he told them to go home and ask their fathers.

Mercer's School, Leslie (aged 14), first row, extreme left.

It was during his first year at Mercers that Leslie learned a hard moral lesson. He had deliberately cheated by copying from the boy next to him during a maths exam, and was horrified a little while later when he was summoned to the headmaster's office and asked how he had managed to work out his sums. There's no mention of why he was summoned, although it's probably safe to guess that the headmaster was surprised at Leslie's sudden ability in maths given his poor record to date. Leslie's response to the question of how he had managed was simply to lie, and to say that he had written it down on a piece of paper, at which he was told to produce the piece of paper the following day. Using his ingenuity, he wrote down some workings on a piece of scrap paper, crumpled it into a ball and dutifully took it to the headmaster, apologising for its appearance since he had retrieved it from the waste paper basket. The headmaster was taken in, and Leslie was so horrified by the whole experience that he decided never to cheat again. About a year later, he was again summoned to the Head Master's office, entering in fear and trepidation and filled with consternation when the head handed him his father's cheque for the term's tuition and said, "Boy, we won't require this any more!". But alarm immediately turned to joy when he learned that he had been awarded a Kings Scholarship for free tuition, which at that time amounted to £6 per term, plus books!

Leslie worked hard and made good progress at Mercers, although he was still a year or so behind due to his childhood illnesses and the rather haphazard tuition he had received at the prep school. He did extremely well in the Oxford Junior exams, [5] although the fact that he was 16 when his fellow students were 14 or 15 made him feel humiliated. He needn't have been, since it was in that year that his short story, The New Director, appeared in the Mercer's School Magazine, showing talent not only for writing, but also the ability to put together quite a complicated plot. However, this success wasn't enough to compensate for his humiliation at being held back academically, and his frustration was further fuelled when he was informed that he wouldn't be allowed to sit for the Senior Oxford exam for another two years, therefore preventing him from being able to apply for university. Leslie was determined to overcome these obstacles and to succeed, and so, having investigated other ways of furthering his education at a faster pace, he decided to enter himself for the prestigious London University Matriculation Examination, which, if he passed, would enable him to move ahead into Mercer's sixth form, and the possibility of applying to university. Thankfully his parents were agreeable, and although the Headmaster at Mercer's gave his permission, his attitude towards Leslie was nevertheless somewhat sarcastic. Fearing further humiliation if he failed, Leslie kept his decision to himself, apart from a close school friend who helped him with physics, a subject in which he had received no tuition at school. Six weeks after the exams, the results were exhibited at South Kensington, and Leslie was so traumatised by the whole event that decades later he still remembered that his entrant number had been 25541. His successful matriculation was a turning point, not only in Leslie's self esteem, since his teachers and classmates were amazed by his success, but also in his progress within the school; he was able to move two years ahead into the sixth form, was appointed as a prefect, and soon became deputy head boy, all of which really gave him the confidence to believe in himself and his capabilities.

The uncle of one of Leslie's school friends, Guy Rothery, was secretary to the Royal Choral Society, and he gifted the Sparey family free seats for several concerts at the Royal Albert Hall. Leslie's interest in music, which had originated in music-making at home, was no doubt stimulated by these precious evenings in the magnificent Albert Hall, as it was also by playing violin and piano duets with his pianist friend Dick Scully.

Between the ages of 14 and 16 Leslie's love for music reached new heights when he developed an intense interest in radio, which as far as the general public was concerned was very much in its infancy. This interest was fired by his friend, Jack Neilson, whose knowledge of electricity and allied sciences was quite advanced for a boy of his age, and together they pooled their pocket money and decided to build some crystal and one-valve radio receivers; at the same time Leslie read almost everything he could lay his hands on about the theory and practice of 'wireless' as it was then known, and practically all his reading time was devoted to the subject of radio and very little else. Herbert was sceptical about the boys' ability to build a receiver, but Amy gave them all the encouragement they needed, despite the fact that they weren't aware of anyone else who either owned or had made a radio. A further complication was that it was illegal for anybody to receive radio messages of any kind, including morse code, and since all receivers required a large aerial rising 20 or 30 feet above ground, constructing one in the garden wasn't something which Herbert was happy to agree to. Before too long, however, he became more cooperative and bought a large flag pole with aerial attached, which he erected at the bottom of the garden; his one proviso was that, in order to avoid prosecution, the aerial must be let down during day-light hours in case it was noticed by the police.

With the project now positively encouraged by his father, Leslie set about constructing his first receiver set; the process involved was not for the fainthearted, for it required not only time but meticulous precision and a steady hand. For more than three hours he carefully wound dozens of yards of copper wire around a large cardboard cylinder, aware that should he for a moment have lost his concentration and inadvertently let go of the wire, it would have sprung free and taken flight all over the room. Thankfully this initial stage was successful, and at last he was able to connect the receiver to his headphones and wait anxiously for a signal; but all he could hear was silence. No doubt aware of his disappointment, Amy offered to take his place, and a few minutes later she cried out, "Leslie, Leslie, a signal!". Although what she was hearing was just Morse Code, it wasn't long before Leslie was able to listen to voices, mostly to 2LO [6] as it was known, which at the time was the only experimental station in London. Leslie's next step was to design small crystal receivers which fitted neatly into cigar boxes, and as news spread of his successful venture some of his friends began ordering 'radios' from him.

A little while later Leslie and Jack built their first valve receiver, enjoying the thrill of being able to extend their reception first to France, and then even further afield. Such was their success that they planned to become involved with amateur transmission, although unfortunately this wasn't possible since neither of them was old enough to qualify for a license. Leslie's ultimate ambition of making radio his career was soon discouraged by his science teacher who assured him that since there weren't likely to be any openings in that field it wouldn't be a viable way of earning a good living. Hindsight would no doubt have proved otherwise, of course.

It was during one of Leslie's radio experiments with Jack, surrounded by wires and a mountain of paraphernalia, that Leslie happened to tune into some glorious music which he later described as seeming "to glow like sunshine" and which was part of the opera, Die Meistersinger, composed by Richard Wagner. Suddenly coming across such wonderful sounds was a complete revelation to Leslie, and it was the catalyst for his decision to make music a major part of his life. According to Leslie's memoirs music wasn't included on the syllabus at Mercers, which obviously hadn't deterred musical families from sending their children to the school, for one of the students was an extremely talented musician who frequently played the organ at school assemblies; his name was W.S Lloyd Webber, later to become the father of Andrew Lloyd Webber, composer of the music for shows such as Evita, Cats, and Jesus Christ Superstar. [7]

Leslie's next personal musical ambition was to learn the cello, but Herbert was very discouraging, believing that it would be pointless since he hadn't progressed very far on the violin; however, something must have persuaded Herbert to change his mind, because for his next birthday Leslie was surprised to receive a cello, complete with a tutor book. A little while later Herbert arranged for him to have lessons with an old friend of his, Frederick Bowen, who advertised himself as being 'certified first class in Honours, Society of Arts, and R.A.M.' (Royal Academy of Music). There's no doubt that Bowen was a man of multi-musical talents, not only teaching a variety of instruments, but also running junior and senior orchestras in his old Victorian house near Finsbury Park, Herbert taking part on the violin, Leslie on the cello, and his friend Dick Scully on the piano. Leslie's progress on the cello must have been fairly rapid, for before long he and Dick were ploughing their way through the cello repertoire, Dick's advanced technique dragging Leslie along as he battled to keep up. Leslie also played in a piano trio with Herbert and another friend, obviously attempting less challenging music, since they were often involved in playing at concerts as well as providing music for local dramatic productions.

During his years at Mercers Leslie occasionally attended concerts, particularly Promenade concerts at the Queen's Hall under the renowned conductor, Sir Henry Wood. But Leslie was a critical listener, and he found that he needed to hear some music several times before he could appreciate it. He was keen to hear the four Brahms symphonies, but on attending a performance of the second symphony he was so disappointed and bored that he compared the music to "exercises for the orchestra!". All was not lost, however, for having listened to the work several times he was "completely won over". On another occasion Leslie and Dick heard a performance of On Hearing the First Cuckoo in Spring by Frederick Delius, in their opinion such dreadful music that they bought a record of it in order to play it to their friends, and forcing them to listen to it since it was "supposed to be music!". As with the Brahms symphony, further hearings of the Delius completely changed their opinion, and finally they were enchanted.

Due to a few unfortunate experiences opera was a form of music which Leslie had already decided to avoid. As a young boy he had been exposed to several oratorio performances which he had found so boring that his endurance had been sorely tested; he never forgot the experience of sitting through a concert featuring parts of Handel's Messiah in the local Congregational Church and of being given some cake in order to stop him fidgeting. His opinion changed dramatically when, at the age of 17, he attended a performance of Gounod's Faust given by a second-rate travelling opera company who were visiting the local theatre for a week; Leslie was so excited by the whole experience that he was unable to sleep that night, going again the following evening in order to hear Bizet's opera, Carmen. This was the beginning of what was to become a life-long love of opera.

Having successfully passed his matriculation and graduated to the sixth form at Mercers, Leslie was fast approaching the vital question of what path his future should take. There were almost endless possibilities, and he was extremely fortunate in having a father who told him that he should choose whatever career he wanted, his one stipulation being, "within reason". Herbert's encouragement was given despite the fact that there were no state grants in England at that time, and Leslie obediently went ahead and wrote down every possible career that interested him, sending away for the brochures and prospectuses; after a long process of elimination the subjects he was left with were medicine, science, music and journalism, in that order of preference. Regarding his first choice he decided to consult the family doctor, and was referred on to a heart specialist who advised against a medical career on the grounds that a doctor's life would be far too strenuous, given his medical history. Having put some initial disappointment behind him, Leslie turned his attention to his second choice, physics, but this too was met with a negative response when he was told by his science teacher that there was no future for physicists unless he was prepared to go and work in Germany. This was an understandable reaction at the time, since no-one was able to predict what the future held for research in physics, and even more particularly, electronics.

Totnes 1923, Elsie, Amy, Leslie, Herbert.

Still focusing on science, Leslie decided to turn instead to analytical chemistry, which required him to take the Inter B.Sc exam, (probably the equivalent of the A level exam) involving chemistry, physics, maths and biology. This was a two-year course which Leslie decided to pack into one, much against the advice of his tutors, and indeed, as the year passed he felt that he was being tested to his limits. Ironically, personal tuition for advanced maths was given by the senior master at Mercers, who just few years earlier had called his student "a blithering idiot"; this new stage in their student/tutor relationship was obviously very positive, because it led to a good and lasting friendship. Since there was no biology department at Mercers, Leslie travelled to Birkbeck College, part of London University, where he was particularly impressed by the professor of botany, the rather formidable Dame Helen Gwynne-Vaughan, a prominent English botanist and mycologist and one of the greatest authorities on fungi. One of the requirements of the biology course was keeping a sketchbook, and since Leslie's drawing skills weren't particularly good, this was something which he found extremely demanding. Despite the challenges and rigorous regime of the course, Leslie was relieved when he successfully passed his final exams, a success which undoubtedly put him in good stead for what was very soon to become his future career, for it was whilst he was studying at Birkbeck that the family dentist suggested that he might consider dentistry. Such a thought had never even occurred to Leslie, especially since he could hardly bear the thought of spending the rest of his life "looking into mouths", but when he discovered that it was possible to take both dental and medical training at the same time he saw an opportunity for fulfilling his real ambition of becoming a doctor.

Leslie visited and gained interviews in all the five London medical colleges with dental schools at that time; during an interview at University College the Principal asked him what sports he played, and having handled a racquet a few times Leslie replied, "tennis", at which the Principal shouted, "I said sport, not pat ball!". In the end he decided that the London Hospital Medical College and Dental School in the East End of the city was his best option, since it was by far the easiest to reach by tram or bus; having passed the necessary entrance exams in biology and chemistry, he entered the College early in 1927, at the age of 18.

Leslie's sister Elsie was still living in the family home during Leslie's years at Mercer's college; she was extremely fond of her younger brother, having nurtured his education during their years living out in Staines, and no doubt she was keen to see him happy and successful in whatever life path he chose to follow. Shortly before he began his studies at the London Hospital Medical College, Elsie married her fiancé, Wallis Roach, moving out of 24 Dunsmure Road, and initially settling down somewhere in North London. It was the end or an era and the start of a new one for Herbert and Amy, as they said goodbye to their daughter and prepared to see their son through a vital period of his young life.

Chapter Five

Taking the future in hand

There were no state grants when Leslie began his medical studies, but thankfully the Mercers' Company awarded him a Rich Exhibition of £200, with Herbert agreeing to pay all the fees, as well as providing a set of dental instruments, a foot drill, two human sculls and all the necessary textbooks. The London Hospital was the largest teaching hospital in Britain at the time, and world famous for its surgery; Leslie remembered being quite overawed as he began his training, and although he found the East End of London rather depressing with its extreme poverty and slums, he was fascinated by its cosmopolitan inhabitants - Jews, Chinese, Africans and Indians.

And so began Leslie's strenuous training in both medicine and dentistry, his time taken up with lectures and practical work during the day, and with studying at home during the evening; unlike universities with their long summer breaks, there were virtually no holidays for the students at the London Hospital, the practical courses continuing throughout the year. Needless to say, when in his final year Leslie found himself suffering from chronic exhaustion, his doctor was amazed to learn that his patient had hardly stopped studying since beginning his studies.

During his first year Leslie's studies included anatomy, dental technology and the making of artificial dentures, as well as working in Surgical Out Patients; he was also introduced to the initial stages of hands-on dentistry, and found the work he was required to do in his patients' mouths extremely unpleasant to begin with.

Studying medicine and dentistry at the same time was an enormous undertaking, and it wasn't long before Leslie began to find it too much to cope with; on consulting the Dean of the College he was advised to temporarily drop the medical course, and to resume after qualifying as a dentist some three years later.

The second year of training introduced the dental students to various dental techniques, including gold inlays, root fillings, and use of the foot drill, all practised on a 'phantom head' which was erected at the top of a dental chair. It was once these techniques had been well honed that the students began having more contact with live patients, including the introduction of tooth extraction, which was initially well supervised. Leslie's first experience was thankfully easy enough, and since he felt that it was a really historic occasion he was keen to remember his patient's name, which just happened to be Mr. Spitting! At that time dental extraction was often administered with the patient under a general anaesthetic, which needed to be efficiently planned and organised since the dentist only had half to one and a half minutes to extract anything from one to several teeth; not only that, but dental students were required to operate in full view of an audience, consisting of House Surgeon in charge, the anaesthetist, several students and the attending nurse, who was known as Sister Dental.

All teaching hospitals depended on charities for

their enormous expenses, and it was customary for medical students to run a collection rag day [8] every Christmas; Leslie's involvement was one of the least pleasant experiences of his years as a student. Dressed in "outrageous attire" he was posted, with his collection box, to London Bridge station, right next to Guys Hospital, which was the London Hospital's main opposition in sport, especially rugby. After early morning success with generous commuters, a cry of alarm warned the students that they were being attacked by a hoard of students from Guys, swooping in on all sides and taking some London Hospital students prisoner, including Leslie. Having marched them to Guys, they were lined up with feet tied together and given a mock tribunal, before being covered in paint and marched in a procession over London Bridge, Leslie terrified that the jeering Guys' students would throw them all into the River Thames. On reaching the Monument they were bundled into taxis and, still tied together, sent back to the London Hospital. This incident caused serious problems with the governing bodies of the London Hospital, since some of the money had been lost in the mayhem, poor Leslie finding himself in the position of having to give evidence before the Chairman, Lord Knutsford.

All in all, Leslie didn't find his years as a dental student very easy socially; he wasn't able to take part in sports, he didn't smoke or drink alcohol, and wasn't particularly interested in the opposite sex, which was probably a bounty in disguise since fraternising between male students and the five hundred or so nurses was forbidden. At that time all medical and dental students were men, with the Royal Free being the only hospital in London to accept women. Leslie's interest in music no doubt helped him to cope with the challenges of student life, and he was particularly interested in chamber music, something which he was able to nourish by attending St. Catherine's Cree Church in the City, where at lunch time every Wednesday a ladies' quartet performed repertoire by Haydn, Mozart and Beethoven. Such was Leslie's enthusiasm that he tried to form a Chamber Music Society at the London Hospital, but without success. Any spare moment was devoted to cello playing, and although he continued to have lessons from Mr. Bowen, it wasn't until a few years later that he decided to take his technique to a much higher level.

It was probably at this time that Leslie and his friend Dick Scully began attending Covent Garden Opera House, and the only way they were able to afford their visits was by sitting up in the amphitheatre, often referred to as the gods; booking seats involved arriving at the Opera House at 6am in order to put down small camp chairs which were on hire for sixpence each, and then returning to them by 5pm. The seats in the amphitheatre were very uncomfortable, with only one or two rows having seat-backs to them; people unlucky enough to have an unbacked seat would tentatively try leaning against the knees of the person behind, and depending on how generous that person was, the knees either stayed put or were withdrawn rapidly! Nevertheless, Leslie was enthralled by his visits to the Opera House, later commenting that "there was something intangible and magic about Covent Garden, the gradual lowering of the lights, the hushed audience, the slight glow from the orchestral pit, the raised baton for the first chord of the overture, the raising of the massive curtain". During later life Leslie often spoke of attending one of the first performances of Stravinsky's ballet, The Rite of Spring, choreographed by the great Russian, Diaghilev, of the Ballet Russes; and he recollected with great humour how he and Dick participated in the general pandemonium which the performance generated due to the modern music and the strange new dance steps. However, since the first performances took place in 1913, with a second production in Paris in 1920, Leslie's memory can't have served him correctly, and it's more than probable that what they actually attended was the redesigned production of the Stravinsky/Diaghilev ballet, The Firebird, at the Lyceum Theatre, London, in November 1926. There were other musical delights to be savoured when time and funds permitted, although he only referred to one or two during conversations, little realising that many of his concert and theatre experiences would later be considered as historic; for instance, his reference to hearing the great Russian opera singer, Feodor Ivanovich Chaliapin, gave no clue as to what he was singing or where, and only through research is it possible to discern that in all probability it was his appearance at the London Lyceum in May 1931, as part of the Russian Season directed by Sir Thomas Beecham. Chaliapin's most famous part was the title role of Mussorgsky's Boris Godunov, excerpts of which he actually recorded in 1929-31, covering the period when Leslie would have heard him sing it.

After nearly five years of intensive study, Leslie finally qualified as a dental surgeon in 1931 at the age of 23, having been awarded the London Hospital Prize in Orthodontics. He was glad to be able to move on, for despite family support and his interest in music as a much-needed outlet, he had always felt like a fish out of water at the hospital, the few friends with whom he shared common interests there being mostly Indian and South African. His intention had been to practise dentistry initially, completing his medical degree a little later, but in the end this didn't happen; ironically, since he never cancelled his official registration, a place at the London Hospital medical school was open to him for the rest of his life.

Leslie having qualified as a dentist, 1931.

Leslie qualified during what was one of the worst

economic depressions in history, affecting poor and rich countries alike; millions were unemployed as personal income, tax revenue, profits and prices dropped, while international trade plunged by more than fifty percent. Although the Dentists' Act had been passed ten years earlier, in 1921, seventy percent of dentists on the register were still unqualified or unregistered, and at least initially they were allowed to carry on, despite the fact that there were some who, according to Leslie, "were appalling". Soon after qualifying Leslie managed to find some half-day locum jobs, most of them in the East End of London, and in Chingford where he became friends with the main dentist there, later to become one of Leslie's patients. The contrast between being a student and a qualified dentist was dramatic; gone was the supervision and the checking, although Leslie soon proved himself more than capable when he had to manage one of the worst cases of dental haemorrhage he had encountered to date. Then, after a few weeks, came the big breakthrough, when Leslie was appointed as a Dental House Surgeon to the London Hospital, and although the salary was very low, the honour and experience more than compensated. From being a student a few weeks earlier he found himself in charge of a whole department of dental students, approving and signing for their work, demonstrating and teaching, as well as attending to the nine hundred or so medical and surgical inpatients who needed dental treatment during his time there; being rather a reticent person and possessing an inferiority complex, this appointment was a major turning point in Leslie's life.

Chapter Six

Facing responsibility

Shortly after his tenure finished an unexpected opportunity arose through the recommendation of the Librarian of the British Dental Association, Mrs. Lindsay, an elderly lady who was the first woman in Britain to qualify; she introduced Leslie to a Mr. Booth, a dental surgeon based in Scunthorpe, who was in hospital in London awaiting an operation to be followed by a long convalescence. He was looking for a locum to cover his practice for several months, and on interviewing Leslie at his bedside asked him, amongst other questions, how much he expected to be paid every week; bracing himself, Leslie bravely mentioned the figure of seven pounds, at which Mr. Booth snapped, "Who the devil do you think you are? It will be six pounds or nothing." Leslie accepted the offer, and within a few days he was on a train travelling to the north of England.

Scunthorpe was one of the most important and largest steel processing centres in Britain, and as a result it was unaffected by the economic depression which hit Britain during the 1930s. The night skies were still aglow with the red hue of the blast furnaces during Leslie's time there, and he was impressed by a visit he made to the factory, where he was able to watch the molten steel "being poured out like hot soup, and rolled out into plates or railway lines". Leslie was the only qualified dentist in Scunthorpe, and his assistant, Kathleen, had had no formal training; not long after he began practising, Leslie was alarmed to discover that he was expected to give general anaesthetics (nitrous oxide or 'gas') as well as extracting the teeth, and when he asked for a doctor to be present in order to administer the gas, he was told that none of the local doctors had been trained or knew how to do it. Giving general anaesthetics had been a part of Leslie's training, and with the assurance from Kathleen that she knew which knobs to turn on their very old-fashioned machine, Leslie proceeded to be doctor and dentist at the same time. When a very difficult child was due to have a general anaesthetic, Leslie decided to ask the child's doctor to assist, and although he assured Leslie that he would be of no use, he nevertheless attended, albeit taking no notice of what was happening and sitting at the back of the surgery reading the newspaper.

During his residency in Scunthorpe Leslie was fortunate to find some good rented accommodation at the cost of £2 per week, which gave him a balance of £4 to cover all his other needs. The dental technician and his wife, a Mr. and Mrs. Raynor, often invited him to their home during the evenings, no doubt treating him to a good meal before attempting, unsuccessfully, to teach him to play bridge!

Leslie spent his free evenings and weekends in walking and exploring the neighbourhood, times which allowed him to think about the meaning of life, something which had preoccupied him as a teenager during his cycle rides in the countryside. At that time, not long after the end of the First World War, he had thought a great deal about peace and how best to avoid another war, and although he had been brought up as an agnostic, he had finally come to the conclusion that only a religious approach made any sense; with this in mind he had begun to read about world religions, soon narrowing his search to Christianity. This belief was confirmed when, at the age of 14, he had experienced what he later felt must have been the presence of the Holy Spirit as he attended an amateur performance of Jerome K. Jerome's play, The Passing of The Third Floor Back. [9] These thoughts of spiritual meaning and the purpose of life had been with him ever since, and by the time he arrived in Scunthorpe he had made the decision that since he had never been baptised, it was probably something which needed to be rectified. He arranged with the vicar of the old church of Frodingham for the ceremony to take place there, with two people he didn't know from the congregation acting as his sponsors. In a lighter moment Leslie found it quite amusing that of the two parishes in Scunthorpe, which was one of the chief iron and steel manufacturers in Britain, the vicar of one was the Rev. Steel, the other a Rev. Rust!

When Mr. Booth had recovered sufficiently to return to his dental practice he invited Leslie to take up the offer of a joint partnership in his branch practice in a small mining town near Doncaster. However, Leslie declined the offer after having visited the town, and more particularly, the house he would be living in, since coal dust covered every surface, making everything look dismal and black, and giving him a sense of foreboding. It was shortly after this visit that he was suddenly taken ill with acute colitis, and rushed by ambulance to the local hospital; Herbert and

Amy were alerted, and his brother-in-law, Wallis, caught the next train north from London. Fortunately the treatment worked and he was released after a few days, but not before a young nurse came to prepare him for an operation which the doctor had said was unnecessary; Leslie lost no time in telling her that she had made a mistake! The after-affects of the colitis stayed with Leslie for over thirty years, and he always carefully avoided eating anything with pips in.

Shortly after Leslie returned to London in 1933, he began suffering from depression, and although it lasted for several months it never occurred to him that it might be a common complaint and that he could consult a doctor about it. His depression was probably the result of his years of hard studying without a break, coupled with all the stress of the war years and his determined efforts to catch up at school following his childhood illnesses. Thankfully the depression finally lifted of its own accord, and Leslie was able to set his mind to the business of earning his living.

Although there were plenty of dentists in the area of London where Leslie was still living with his parents, he decided nevertheless to set up a private dental practice in the family home in Dunsmure Road, and "hope for the best". Ever the supportive father, Herbert lent him the £500 necessary to equip a first-class practice, and Leslie began converting his old 'nursery' at No. 24 into a modern surgery, purchasing all the latest dental equipment available in Britain at that time; the drawing room with the baby-grand piano became the patients' waiting room, and when after several weeks everything was ready, Leslie hung his bronze plate outside and, "like a spider" in its web, waited for his first victim! He had a long time to wait before a lady arrived for a tooth extraction, and the dentist was as nervous as the patient, realising that a great deal depended upon his early reputation.

The first few weeks were extremely quiet, one patient during the first week, three the week following, and two in the week after that; but the numbers soon started to rise, Leslie's modern dental surgery proving to be quite a showplace and Herbert proudly inviting some of his customers to come and see it! It wasn't long before Leslie was in need of a receptionist or chair-side assistant, and when he placed an advert in the Telegraph he was amazed to receive a hundred replies! Having picked out six who lived nearby, Leslie selected 15-year-old Doris Trussler, paying a weekly wage of twelve shillings and sixpence and raising it to fifteen shillings shortly afterwards when she more than proved herself capable. [10] She was a very smart and efficient girl and stayed for three or four years, later becoming one of the founders of The Dental Nurses' Society and training young women to take the recently-formed certificate.

Leslie was determined to make dentistry as painless and fear-free as possible, giving injections for practically all fillings and reducing discomfort to an absolute minimum. Although there was no reason at all why other dentists shouldn't follow the same procedure, very few did, and Leslie's practice grew steadily as a consequence. As his reputation for pain-free treatment spread, patients starting coming from other parts of London as well as from the countryside beyond. During the first year or so he was offered some part-time positions which were extremely useful in helping him build his reputation as well as his bank balance. Once a week he visited the British Dental Hospital, which was a very small charity hospital in the Camden Town district of London; Leslie risked his own health by working there since some of the patients were suffering from tuberculosis and the dental equipment was extremely primitive, which meant that extra care was always needed in the sterilisation of instruments. Of the other positions he accepted, one involved a charity in Stoke Newington which looked after the interests of 'fallen girls' and called itself the London Female Guardian Society, and another was with the London County Council, where he was often expected to treat twenty or more school children in a couple of hours. Something which he considered as a real breakthrough was being appointed by the Metropolitan Police to look after the teeth of the local force.

Leslie's private dental practice at 24 Dunsmure Road brought in patients of all kinds, many of whom he still remembered decades later. One of the first was his local member of Parliament, Sir George Jones, obviously quite a coup for a newly qualified dentist still at the beginning of his career, although not everything went quite to plan initially; as Sir George sat back in the dental chair, Leslie leaned over his shining bald head and told him gently to "Open wide," at which the ceiling decided to descend, covering patient and dentist in fine plaster dust. Sir George was not deterred by this in the least, and on subsequent visits would jokingly ask Leslie how the ceiling was. A lady patient amused her young dentist by bringing to her appointments a clean towel and vest, and disappearing into the bathroom to change as soon as she arrived; there appeared to be no explanation, and if he ever discovered what her reason was, Leslie didn't disclose it. Another patient was terrified of swallowing the cotton wool rolls used to keep teeth dry when being filled, and she insisted that Leslie tie pieces of cotton to each one so that she could hold the other end of the cotton while he was operating. It was just the beginning of a long dental career with never a dull moment.

Leslie with his team in his new dental practice, 14 Dunmore Road.

During his first years in dental practice Leslie engaged his cousin, Reg Epps, as his accountant; many years his senior, Reg refused to take any payment for his services, his reason being that Herbert had been extremely good to him when he was just commencing his own career. This was very helpful to Leslie as he built up his practice, which by the third year had increased from about one patient per week to a hundred. The surgery opened its doors at 9am and in order to accommodate those of his patients who worked in the City, often remained open until 8 o'clock or even later, and until 12.30pm on Saturdays; no doubt by this time the part-time positions were no longer a part of his agenda. It was several years before Leslie's health began to suffer as a result of his excessive and relentless hard work.

A large proportion of patients attending Leslie's practice were Jewish, and not long after setting himself up a very kind Jewish patient advised him that, since the Jews were used to bargaining, he should fix a fair price for their dental work and never be prepared to change it; as a result he never had a bad debt among his Jewish patients. There was always a degree of anti-Semitism, even amongst people who considered themselves Christian, but Leslie had a good relationship with his Jewish neighbours, having had a long association with the Jewish population living around the London Hospital in Whitechapel, as well as in Stamford Hill, where he lived; the building next door to the Sparey home at that time was, in fact, a private synagogue, and the Spareys were often asked to go in on the Sabbath in order to take care of basic tasks which were forbidden to the believers on that day, including blowing out candles and turning off lights.

In 1936 Leslie was appointed as one of Marks and Spencer's team of dental surgeons taking care of their employees in four of the large North London stores; at a time when the National Health Service hadn't been formed, it was a unique dental service, giving Leslie a clear insight into the way that the Jewish-controlled Marks and Spencer's ran its business and cared for the employees. At about this time a Jewish-Christian Society was formed locally in order to try to resolve the difficulties that arose between the Jewish community and its Gentile neighbours, and Leslie was appointed as a representative of the Congregational Church; as time drew nearer to 1939 and the outbreak of the Second World War, this society played an increasingly important roll in dealing with the many problems arising from the almost daily arrival of Central European Jews fleeing from the Nazi terror. It seemed that big challenges were on the horizon, not only for the Jews, but for everyone living at that time.

Chapter Seven

Finding a balance

Before his private dental practice had become well established, Leslie had managed to find time to spare between patients during which he was able to develop his various interests. Since he wasn't affiliated with a church or involved in any sports activities he found it difficult to connect with other young people, and although he hired a tennis coach Leslie soon realised that however long he tried, he would never make any progress with the game, something which the coach was too polite to mention! Joining the local amateur dramatic society was more encouraging, and he was pleased to be offered the part of a rather silly farm-hand in their latest production, Eden Phillpot's Yellow Sands. His rendition was obviously successful, for a few days later it was reported that a lady in the audience had said to a friend, "That yokel is, I understand, a young dentist who has just started practising nearby; I won't go to him, he is obviously barmy!". Leslie also found time to practise his cello, and later, when he could afford to, he began taking lessons at Trinity College of Music with Austrian cellist Ludwig Lebell, who had studied with Popper and Bruckner at the Vienna Conservatoire before settling in England, and who was also a prolific composer of cello music. Another interest Leslie was keen to nurture was preservation of the countryside, and he decided to become a member of the first committee of the Hampden Society, named after John Hampden, who was the romantic hero of the Civil War. [11] Unfortunately the society was short-lived, but whilst it was functioning Leslie thoroughly enjoyed his trips by train into the Buckinghamshire countryside. In about 1935 Herbert bought Leslie his first car, a new Austin 10, at the cost of £400 or so; motoring was still somewhat of a novelty, and driving tests were a thing of the future, Leslie making do with some basic instructions from the car salesman and a few informal lessons from friends before venturing out into the nearby countryside in days when it was rare for the average city-dweller to venture far from home territory.

Leslie and Herbert.

With lingering memories of the Great War Leslie was preoccupied by the question of how to make the world a safer and better place a reality for the future, and it was as a result of this preoccupation that he began working for the League of Nations Union. (See *Appendix 1*) At the local level, the object was to educate the public about world affairs through lectures, meetings and conferences, and shortly after Leslie joined the local 'North Hackney' branch he was told that the Youth Group had ceased to function, and asked if he would be prepared to reorganise it and if possible bring it back to life. Believing that this was something he could manage, Leslie jumped at the opportunity, with the feeling that at last he might conceivably "contribute a drop in the ocean towards the peace of the world".

Setting about his task with enthusiasm, Leslie gathered together as many young people as possible, formed a committee, and was elected as honourable secretary. With chairman, treasurer and social secretary in place, a programme of events and meetings was soon in full swing, including lectures, discussions, occasional dances, and rambling in the nearby countryside, with everything neatly printed on attractive Junior Members' Cards. Quite by chance Leslie came into contact with two people who were to feature in his future personal life; the first of these was a committee member of the main branch of the Union, a Mr. Rolls, who represented the local Methodist Church, and whose granddaughter Leslie would marry just a few years later; the other, a young man by the name of Donald Powles, served on the same committee as Leslie, and was first cousin to the same young lady. But during his initial connection with the League all Leslie's energies were focused on its success, particularly that of the youth group, which went from strength to strength.

When Leslie was invited to represent North Hackney on the London Region Federation he found himself involved in organising national conferences, including those at Hoddesden, Malvern, and Eastbourne, as well as attending an international youth conference in Geneva. He was impressed by the quality of the discussions and lectures, and felt that many of those speaking had "real first-hand experience of the world". Those involved had few illusions about the difficulties facing them; the basis of hope was known as 'collective security', the plan being that if one of the fifty or so member states were attacked, then all the others would go to its assistance. In the end, fear and short-sighted national interest caused its failure, but at the time there was great hope that the world would become a much safer place.

In 1934 a nation-wide questionnaire, known as the Peace Ballot, was circulated in order to find out what the people's attitude was to the League of Nations and collective security. Although it was an unofficial ballot, by the time the vote was counted and announced in June 1935, thirty-eight percent - eleven and a half million people - had voted in favour. Leslie had helped in collecting ballot papers after the vote, and attended a large gathering at the Royal Albert Hall where amongst the several distinguished speakers was an elderly man sitting at the back of the platform who spoke at the end of the meeting. Tapping Leslie's shoulder, one of his friends said, "that is Winston Churchill; he's quite old now, he was very famous once, but of course he's had his day." Little did they realise how the very future of Britain, and indeed, Europe, would soon depend on that old man's leadership. Despite the positive result of the ballot and the desire of the general populace to avert war at all costs, Hitler had already been making moves and flexing his muscles as early as 1934, and not long after the result of the ballot was announced Mussolini began his attack on Abyssinia.

Some of Leslie's friends in the League began hinting that perhaps he should be thinking of his future, and start looking for a wife. He had decided years earlier that when he married, the girl he chose must be keen on music, since it was such an important part of his life. He had been friendly with only a few girls and taken one or two to a concert or to the cinema, but had never found them interesting or musical enough to pursue. Not long after starting his dental practice Leslie began attending the local Congregational Church, whose minister, the Rev. Henry Donald, had a keen interest in contemporary issues and international affairs. One Sunday as he sat to the back of the church Leslie noticed an attractive young girl sitting in front of him with a young man, and was disappointed that she seemed to have a boy friend, later learning that he was, in fact, her father, then aged about 40. Leslie had no idea who the young girl was, and such was his interest that his church attendance became more frequent!

The following spring the church held a music competition, and Leslie went along to hear some of the competitors. The 16 years and over piano class involved about eight young women playing Schumann's Aufschwung, and to Leslie's delight, number five was the girl he had been admiring from afar; impressed by her playing, his interest was roused even further. Here was not only a beautiful girl, but a musical girl, and her name appeared in the programme. It was Joan Rolls, and Leslie had no doubt that he wanted to make her acquaintance.

Chapter Eight

Rolls family roots and early beginnings

Before moving to the London area the Rolls family had originated in the West Country of England, as had the Spareys. Joan's great grandfather Charles was a coach builder in Dorset, and his son Thomas was born in Blandford Camp in the year 1859. During his first years of employment Thomas earned his living as a 'letter sorter', although by the census of 1911, when he and his large family were living in Stoke Newington, London, he had been promoted to the position of 'Senior assistant GPO'. His wife was Susan Allingham from Islington, whom he had married on December 25th 1880, and over the following twenty years of their marriage they had moved house several times as the family expanded. [12] By 1911 Thomas and Susan had eight children, and although the six who were old enough to be married were still single and living at home, they were all contributing to the household expenses, working variously as clerks and showroom assistants.

Stanley, who was to become Joan's father, was child number seven; he was 15 years old at the time of the 1911 census, no doubt beginning to think of his future and little dreaming that within three years he would be fighting in the Great War. When war broke out at the beginning of August, 1914, he was 18 years and 11 months old, and working as a clerk for the British Legal Insurance Company; just a week later, on August 11th he enlisted with the Territorial Force of the County of London, agreeing to serve his country for four years with the 10th County of London Battalion. Now knowing what conditions were like for those who bravely fought during the Great War, it's not surprising that Stanley never spoke of his wartime experiences, which included the horrific Sulva Bay landing at Gallipoli during August 1915. When he contracted dysentery and tuberculosis he was moved to a hospital in Malta, later discharged and sent back to England. Sadly, his elder brother, Thomas Albert, died at the Battle of Loos in Northern France, sometime in September 1915.

The Rolls family. Thomas and Susan Rolls, centre, their son Stanley with his wife, Dorothy, top left. Joan, bottom row, second from the right.

Where and when Stanley met Dorothy Webb isn't recorded, and although little is known of Dorothy's father, William Robert Webb - apart from the fact that he was born about 1855 in Little London, Hampshire, England - the history of her mother's family is extremely well documented. Sometime in the mid 18th century, Samuel Carter, a shoemaker from Wiltshire, arrived in London. His son, also named Samuel, was also a shoemaker, and when his first wife died, he married Margaret Finch, who sadly died shortly after giving birth to their son George, in 1829. George began his working life apprenticed as a journeyman [13] hatter, and when his apprenticeship ended he set himself up as a journeyman silk hat maker, selling to the wholesale trade from his small cottage on the Old Kent Road, in South East London.

In 1851 George married Sarah Venner, and shortly afterwards they moved to a larger house at 215, Old Kent Road, where George was able to exhibit his hats in a case erected in the front garden, customers climbing a set of steps to the parlour in order to buy his wares. The business was extremely successful, and as a result George decided to build a shop over the front garden, with a giant model of a silk hat erected at the top; by the time of the 1871 census George is noted as employing '2 men 2 boys', and as the business thrived several properties were purchased on either side of the original shop, forming what soon became a clothing store for men's retail and bespoke tailoring, focused particularly on the juvenile trade. The model of a silk hat was replaced by a large clock topped by a bowler hat which rose and fell at 1pm every day, becoming a familiar landmark for the people living in the district, who would set their watches by it. By the year 1901 there were more than thirty-five Carter shops in and around London.

George and Sarah were blessed with eight sons and three daughters; although not the final child, Caroline was the last daughter, born in around 1861, and George, obviously keen to keep her at home, offered to pay for her living if she would take on the role of housekeeper and look after the household. But Caroline had other ideas, and in 1885 she decided to marry her sweetheart, William Robert Webb. William was an electrician in the Crouch End area of London, and although not much is known about his family background, we do know that in 1893 he travelled to the USA in order to visit the 'Chicago World's Fair' (World's Columbian Exhibition). This extravagant celebration of American culture and society was the last of the 19th century's World Fairs, the first of which had taken place at the Crystal Palace, London, in 1851. Visitors travelled from nineteen countries, assured that they would find in Chicago commercial opportunities, entertainment, and a window on the age in which they were living as the new century beckoned. On reaching the east coast of America, William Webb would probably have travelled west by the 'Exposition Flyer', a Pullman coach which managed a speed of 80 miles per hour. Nothing is known regarding William's visit to Chicago, except that he took home a beautiful ivory brooch engraved with the name, Caroline. [14]

Concerning family matters, Caroline apparently followed the example of her parents, although she did restrict the number of children to nine, rather than eleven. Husband William died in 1906, leaving Caroline as head of the family home; all the children were still living at home

The Webb family, taken at the time of Edward VII's coronation.
Front row: mother, Caroline, extreme left, father, William, extreme right.
Dorothy Venner Rolls (mother of Joan), next to William.

with her at this time, and remained with her at least until
1911, when they all appear on the census as being resident
in Islington. Caroline's daughter Dorothy, who was the
middle child, was 16 by this time, and working as a typist,
most probably in a bank. Family hearsay has it that Dorothy
met Stanley Rolls shortly before the beginning of the war,
the relationship no doubt flowering when Stanley returned
from his convalescence on the island of Malta. When
their marriage was registered in the third quarter of 1918,
Dorothy was already pregnant, and despite the ravages of
the war, despite the relief of welcoming home one son regardless of the terrible odds, it seems that neither Stanley's
parents nor Dorothy's were prepared to accept that a baby
had been conceived out of wedlock. This made a difficult
time extremely wretched for the young couple, added to

which during her pregnancy, Dorothy was struck down with the dreaded Asian flu which was killing thousands as it swept the country. As 1919 dawned, the future looked extremely bleak for newly married Mr. and Mrs. Rolls.

Stanley Rolls recovering from tuberculosis on the island of Malta, following his service at Gallipoli.

Chapter Nine

Joan Rolls - the early years

Joan Rolls was born on 17th March 1919 in the Mothers' Hospital of the Salvation Army, Hackney [15]; not long afterwards, both Stanley and Dorothy's parents relented and the families were reunited. Given the difficulties Stanley had had in finding a job and supporting his new family, acceptance from those around them must have been a great relief. Stanley eventually found work as an agent on a housing estate in Tottenham, taking care of all the repairs and maintenance, and being provided with a small flat in St John's Road.

Thankfully Joan agreed to note down her early memories many decades later, offering brief snapshot glimpses both of her daily life and some of the people she shared it with. She began life sleeping in a drop-side cot in her parents' bedroom, and remembered the delight she took in standing up in it and shaking the slatted sides until she could hear someone approaching, at which point she quickly lay down and pretended to be asleep. When she was given her own bedroom with a painted iron bedstead she loved the wallpaper "with great swags of lilac hanging from the top of the wall" and enjoyed lying in bed amongst such "lovely flowers"; Stanley even had a washbasin installed in her room so that she could have a degree of privacy. Every evening a man lit the street gas lamps, and Joan found the light coming from the lamp outside her bedroom window very comforting since she was frightened of the dark; she was also frightened of the "shouts and screams" coming from the street late at night as people made their way home from the pubs.

Dorothy with Joan, aged 10 weeks.

Joan's life was extremely disciplined as a small child, with bedtime strictly at 6pm, and no contact allowed with other children living close by, Dorothy firmly reminding her daughter that they were common, whereas she certainly wasn't; common or not, little Joan looked at them enviously from her bedroom window on summer evenings, and longed to join them. In later life she often referred to Dorothy's rather challenging method of gaining attention and compliance, which involved Joan having to say "bedience" whenever her mother shouted "O"; seemingly it was extremely effective! Whatever Dorothy's reasons for such discipline, she was a very loving mother, and any time Joan suffered inwardly, she was able to find solace in her father, who was very gentle and undemanding. Being a single child long before the era of television and the internet, Joan made her own amusements, losing herself in her own particularly vivid imagination, which included a make-believe friend who was crippled, and who she carried around on her back. The flat in St John's Road was small but adequate; in the living room was a black leaded range with cooker attached, and since there was no bathroom Joan was bathed in a tin bath in front of the living room fire. When Stanley later installed a square bath behind the kitchen door there was much excitement, and Joan remembered how her mother enjoyed the luxury of it. The 'lavatory' was virtually part of the kitchen, although there was a window and a door. Joan loved the cavernous cupboard in the kitchen, to be lifted into it "as into an Aladdin's cave" and to savour the wonderful scents of cinnamon and ginger.

At the rear of the flat was a flight of very steep stairs which when Joan was little Dorothy had negotiated with pram and baby, only once losing her balance and landing at the bottom, all intact and no-one injured. The stairs led down into their tiny private garden which Stanley cultivated with great care, sowing a pocket-size lawn and creating an even smaller rockery. Joan's job was to gather together all the snails, and when Stanley asked her what she had done with them she told him that she had "thrown them over into the next door garden!". To her delight, Joan discovered that it was possible to access the flat beneath them from the garden, and on her illicit visits she was sometimes offered egg and bacon; the husband was a piano tuner, and the son, considerably older than Joan, was of great interest to her. But most of the time in her very early years, Joan was expected to amuse herself, and since she was blessed with a vivid imagination she was able to immerse herself in her own little world. One of her greatest pleasures was to wash the slats on a green latticed door in the garden, and to watch the colour come to life when it was wet; and she loved to scrape the bricks on the back wall, gathering the various colours in a container and mixing them together, although when her parents noticed holes appearing in the wall they soon put a stop to her activity. When she was a little older Joan had a passion for bowling her hoop, going out before breakfast and pushing it along the pavement with a small wooden stick; she also loved playing tennis against a brick wall on the opposite side of the street, practising serving and backhand to her heart's content until the people who lived on the other side of the wall complained of the noise; however, as soon as she saw them leave the house she started again.

At the age of 5 Joan began attending the Board School [16] at the edge of the estate. The school building seemed terrifyingly vast, and she was so frightened as she approached on her first day that she needed to call at a nearby house in order to use their facilities. On entering the classroom for the first time she was amazed by the forty to fifty young faces, by the "variety of human nature"; she was fascinated by a girl whose nose ran constantly, by a boy with a bright red face, and by the girl who wet herself in front of all her class mates. Joan was already able to read by the time she began school; she was introduced to counting and elementary arithmetic with the aid of building blocks, and she always remembered how much she loved the colour of the pale blue chalk which was used on the blackboard. One day Joan was chosen to take tea to the headmistress in her office; she was thrilled, and no doubt a little nervous, for she tripped over some steps and broke the cup. She was horrified by what she had done, and although she felt that she had to tell her parents, she couldn't muster the courage; having spent a long night worrying about it, she finally plucked up the courage to tell her mother, who hardly reacted at all, much to Joan's relief.

Rolls family gathering at Clapton. Joan, centre,
Stanley and Dorothy to her left.

Not long after starting school Joan faced her first real test when she had to go into hospital for a hernia operation; it was the first time she had been separated from her parents, and decades later she still remembered the sensation of being abandoned in a strange and frightening environment. Her fear was eased slightly when she was told that she would be going into a theatre, although when she realised that she wouldn't be seeing a play in the theatre the feeling of unease returned. The anaesthetic was a "horrible experience - almost like being suffocated," she later recalled; her face was burned by it, adding to her misery, and the nausea and sickness left her with a horror of it for the rest of her life. The ward had open fires which needed constant attention, and was full of elderly ladies who made a point of spoiling their young companion, inviting her to sing and recite poetry to them and making a fuss of her on her 6th birthday; when one of the ladies died during the night Joan was kept awake by the noise and bustle as the nurses dealt with the situation. Joan hid her fear and misery from everyone during her stay in hospital, and as soon as she went home she suffered a slight breakdown, which resulted in bouts of sleepwalking over the following years.

Joan and Dorothy reading in their home at St. John's Road.

Joan was 7 when she began attending Our Lady's Convent School at 14, Amherst Park, involving a long walk there and back from her home in St John's Road. Two years earlier the headmistress of the school, Mother Mary Angela Butler, had obtained recognition by the Board of Education and Grant Aid from the London County Council, ensuring the future status and financial stability of the school, and no doubt making good education available to families who otherwise may not have been able to afford it. Joan was more interested in making her friends laugh than in learning, although she was grateful for her English teacher who opened up the world of literature and poetry, which Joan loved passionately for the remainder of her life. Two of Joan's most exciting memories of her time at Our Lady's were listening to the nuns as they sang on their way to chapel, and groping her way to school during the notorious thick London smogs.

Joan didn't explain how it was that she began having regular piano lessons, whether it was something which girls of her age were expected to do, or just an interest which her parents allowed her to take up. There was a steady succession of piano teachers, the first being a Mr. Heep who, according to his young pupil, wasn't very good at all, the second making Joan nervous by setting up student concerts in her living room, the third a Miss Bones who was apparently more than acceptable, and the fourth, a Miss Floyd, who had once been a student of Tobias Matthay, teacher of Myra Hess and Harriet Cohen, and whose efforts twenty years later helped towards enabling the appointment of women as examiners for the Associated Board of the Royal Schools of Music. Miss Floyd booked the Wigmore Hall every year for her student concerts, also encouraging them to enter the Westminster and North London music festivals, and although Joan struggled with nerves, she did win a beautiful bust of Beethoven, a silver medal and a stylish wooden metronome. Whilst at Miss Floyd's Joan made a close and lasting friendship with fellow student Daphne Ibbott, who became one of Britain's finest and best-loved accompanists, and who was to feature in Joan's life many decades later.

Had circumstances been different it's more than probable that Joan would have followed a musical career, such was her talent and musicianship, and although her life took another route, music continued to be an important part of it right to the end, although her battle with performance nerves and self-confidence stayed with her into adulthood.

Minimal recollections and diary notes leave just hints of what was happening during Joan's early years, although it's evident from photos that at some point in her childhood she had a dog, which she named Flannigan. Unfortunately she never explained her reason for choosing the name Flannigan, but it's more than probable that she was inspired by the well-known music hall and vaudeville entertainer, Bud Flanagan, who from 1926 onwards worked as a double act with Chesney Allen. Maybe her parents had attended their performance at the Holborn Empire in 1926. Whatever her reason, Flannigan was obviously much loved, so much so that she dedicated a poem to him when he died:

To Flannigan

My little friend I miss you so
Those happy feet that scampered to and fro
That small damp nose inquisitive, alert
Quite unconscious of the cake of mud and dirt
Acquired while digging in the garden for a bone;
But now my little friend you've left me quite alone,
No walks, no fun, you'll miss those walks as much as I;
Across the fields you loved to fly
With ears cocked catching every sound
Scratching busily at every hole and mound for rabbits.
My little friend I miss your funny ways
Enduring charms that brightened all my days.

Joan with Stanley and her dog, Flannigan. Lady unknown.

Both Dorothy and Stanley's families lived close by, and seemed to be an important part of Joan's social life as she was growing up, any bad feeling due to the circumstances of her birth obviously forgotten. Of her various aunts, Auntie Flo was the one Joan remembered with the most affection,

Joan on holiday at Clackton-on-Sea.

her home in Crouch End always open and welcoming to all the family. Flo's husband, Walter, had fought beside Stanley during the Great War, so the bond was no doubt based on more than simply family ties. Walter worked on the Stock Exchange, often plunging his family into financial embarrassment, but ultimately bringing stability and moderate wealth. Joan remembered her paternal grandfather, Thomas, as being a "dear old man and an ardent Methodist, shy and quiet but very good natured", and her grandmother (Susan) as extremely lively with a keen interest in spiritualism; losing her elder son during the Great War must have weighed heavily on her, and she often told Joan that she could see him in the room.

The annual family holidays when Joan was growing

up were often taken at Clackton-on-Sea, which during the 1920s had become such a popular holiday destination that a new road, the London Road, had been built to cope with the influx of visitors. A handful of photographs of these holidays offer tiny windows into what was seemingly a much-loved yearly event, often spent with a whole community of holiday-makers at Holland House in Skelmersdale Road, just a stone's throw from the beach. Joan often spoke warmly of her childhood friendship with Charles Groves, who also holidayed at Clackton, and who was later to become one of

Joan with Charles Groves.

Britain's best-loved and fêted conductors. [17] Charles had been orphaned when he was just 10 years old, after which he was seemingly brought up by two devoted aunts, who Joan obviously spent time with on her holidays. Although Charles was four years older than Joan they enjoyed a close friendship, which is evident from the few precious photos taken of them together; their mutual love of and involvement in music may have had something to do with their friendship, as too was their shared sense of fun. Charles was in his late teens and Joan still considered a child, but there was never any suggestion of anything inappropriate, simply a sweet friendship. Later holidays were taken at Frinton-on-Sea, a little further along the Essex coast, and by this time Charles had moved on.

Joan aged 16.

When Joan was 16 the family moved from Tottenham to Bush Hill Park, in the Borough of Enfield. But Joan was very sad to be moving away from Tottenham, her main reason being that she was extremely fond of the Minister of the Congregational Church in Stamford Hill, having attended both Sunday and mid-week services on a regular basis. Little did she realise that her presence in the church had already been noticed by a young dentist who admired the Minister for his interest in contemporary issues and international affairs; and little did she realise that her life as a carefree teenager amongst friends and cousins would soon take her in a different direction altogether.

Chapter Ten

The meeting of souls

Joan wore a new green dress for the music competition at the Congregational Church, unaware that as she performed Schumann's Aufschwung a keen admirer in the audience was excitedly noting down her name and competitor number from the programme. Leslie's quest was to discover where his dream girl lived, and by doing some detective work with the help of the telephone directory he eventually discovered a Rolls living in The Meadway, Bush Hill Park. Not quite knowing what his next step should be, he decided to drive over to Joan's street, half hoping that he might see her, although he was to be disappointed. However, all was not lost, for a little while later she appeared at a League of Nations Union garden party with a friend, and as junior secretary Leslie decided to invite her to join the Youth Group; however, Joan was not so easily persuaded, telling him quite offhandedly that she wasn't interested.

One evening Leslie decided to call in on his fellow committee member, Donald Powles, who was just returning from a game of tennis. During the conversation which ensued Donald's mother asked him if Joan Rolls had been there, at which Leslie was so amazed to hear her name being mentioned that he found it difficult to hide his excitement. Calmly, he asked Donald if he knew Joan Rolls, the response being, "Well I ought to, she's my cousin." Soon afterwards Donald invited Leslie to his 21st birthday party, and Leslie was tempted to believe that this could possibly be the breakthrough he needed as he sought an opportunity to finally meet the young woman he was unable to put from his mind. However, even though he had been invited to the party, there was no guarantee that he would have occasion to speak to Joan Rolls, and Leslie realised that what he actually needed was a formal introduction. Donald Powles was one of Leslie's dental patients, and when he made an appointment for a tooth extraction, Leslie decided to use the occasion to mention Joan Rolls; but he was nervous, and as the appointment progressed he put off his question, deciding to speak after the injection, and then, after the extraction, but finding that he was completely tongue tied. In desperation he offered to drive his patient home, and just as Donald was about to leave the car, Leslie quickly asked him if he would introduce him to Joan Rolls at the birthday party. Donald was completely taken aback by this request, and lost no time in reminding Leslie that his cousin was still a young girl; but Leslie quickly recovered himself, cooly responding that he took a great interest in young people who were musical! Apparently Donald agreed to the request.

Leslie's anticipation mounted as the day of the birthday party, November 5th 1935, approached, and finally, when it arrived, he was impatient for it to begin. Donald obediently did as he had been asked, but according to Leslie, making "a most embarrassing hash" of introducing his 16 year-old cousin Joan to his 27 year-old dentist, and no doubt wondering what Leslie's motives could possibly be. As the introduction ended the dance band began playing the

Valeta, at which Leslie escorted Joan around the dance floor. He had made some progress, although what Joan thought at this juncture isn't recorded.

On Monday December 30th they attended the first concert of the 1935/6 Winter Promenade season at the Queen's Hall. It was something Joan had been greatly looking forward to, writing to Leslie a few days earlier in order to tell him that she "was looking forward to the 30th, especially as I have never been to the Queen's Hall before, and I have heard so many wonderful things about Solomon [18] that I am longing to hear him for myself". Unlike the present-day Promenade concerts, the audience was treated to an extremely long programme which included three full works and several short selections, and it was obviously planned in order to suit all tastes. [19] [20]

Despite being a marathon the concert obviously left a deep impression on Joan, who the following Sunday wrote to Leslie, addressing him as Mr. Sparey, and telling him, "I couldn't sleep last Monday night for thinking about the Promenade concert. I have listened to them on the wireless this week, but I don't think you get the same atmosphere in your own home as you do when you are actually there --- do you?" By this time she had obviously reconsidered her decision not to join the League of Nations Union Youth Group, for in the same letter she told him, "you will see that I have enclosed a postal order for a shilling. I suppose I now consider myself a member of the Youth Group."

On February 12th 1936, Joan wrote to Leslie, "Dear Mr. Sparey, I am so glad the weather has turned a bit warmer, my nose is the trouble when it is cold. I seriously thought of making a nose-bag to keep it warm. --- I am looking forward to seeing Romeo and Juliet, it is very nice of you to take me. Yours sincerely, Joan." Leslie had also invited her to accompany him to the League of Nations Youth Group's annual dance in St. Andrew's church hall, Joan tentatively accepting and pointing out that since her home was about 3 miles away she would have difficulty getting home afterwards. Delighted by her acceptance and the opportunity to spend time with the girl of his dreams, Leslie decided to offer her a lift home after the dance, and although Joan accepted, it had first to pass the scrutiny of her mother, who had phoned Donald's mother in order to establish that Leslie was a fit person! Not only did he pass the test, but it appears that Joan was beginning to soften in her attitude towards him, for she wrote him a letter, explaining that on a recent visit to St. Andrew's church hall she noticed that there were two pianos; "I wondered whether you would like my partner and I to play a two-piano duet for the International party," she wrote, continuing, "we won the Silver Medal for this sort of work in December." There is no mention in Leslie's memoirs of whether this actually took place, although it's probably safe to assume that it did.

Joan was still only 16, and there's no record of what she filled her life with at this point, or indeed, if she had even left school. What is sure is that at some point between leaving school and marrying Leslie she spent one term at drama school, something which she hardly ever referred to in later life. The fact that she had auditioned for a place and been accepted showed that she obviously had the talent to pursue acting as a career; however, the stage nerves from which she suffered as a pianist were no doubt also a problem when she attended the drama course, which may be the reason why she didn't stay longer than a term. Or perhaps her budding relationship with Leslie was enough to divert her from contemplating a career at all.

Certainly as far as Leslie was concerned, he never looked back; he had met his dream girl, and she was amenable to accepting his various invitations, no doubt watched closely by her parents. There were two visits to Covent Garden Opera House during 1936; the Grand Opera Season of 1936 at Covent Garden had opened on 27th April with Wagner's Die Meistersinger, conducted by Sir Thomas Beecham and with the principal soprano role being sung by Tiana Lemnitz, a German soprano making her Covent Garden debut. This became Leslie's favourite opera, and he was later proud to admit that in all he saw it seventeen times! The second visit to Covent Garden involved a performance of Tristan and Isolde, after which Joan commented in a letter to Leslie, "I should think your heart did thump when you heard the closing scene --- fancy asking me if I remember it, as if I could forget it; I am so glad you realise how marvellous it is, you didn't really care for it so much before did you?". It would have been surprising if they hadn't been deeply impressed, since not only did the line-up for this production include the world famous singers Lauritz Melchior and Kirsten Flagstad, but the live recording made during performances on May 18th and June 2nd has since been considered the greatest performance to survive in sound. It was during one of these visits to Covent Garden that Leslie was delighted to see, sitting behind them, one of the only two British peers he had ever met, giving him the opportunity to impress Joan by turning round and saying, "Good evening, Lord Allen, may I introduce you to my friend Miss Rolls." Baron Allen of Hurtwood was a politician and prominent pacifist, and it's more than probable that Leslie had met him through his association with the League of Nations Union. If Joan was impressed by being introduced to him, there's no mention of it, although in a letter addressed to 'Leslie' rather than Mr. Sparey on July 2nd she refers to a beautiful book about Covent Garden which he had given her so that she would remember their evenings at the opera; by this time Joan has started signing off, "yours sincerely, Micky."

A few weeks before the Covent Garden visit, Leslie took Joan to Eastbourne for the League of Nations Union Easter conference, arranged by the youth groups, and in particular Leslie's North Hackney branch. During the drive to Eastbourne Leslie managed to engage Joan in such stimulating conversation that by the time they arrived he had no doubt at all that this was the girl he wanted to marry.

The conference was extremely positive, with plenty to discuss as the situation in Europe was steadily deteriorating. The persecution of the Jews in Germany had commenced the previous year, there was trouble brewing between Italy and Abyssinia which had the potential to affect the rest of Europe, and just a month before the Eastbourne conference German military forces had entered the Rhineland; 1936 was also a year of constitutional crisis in Britain, caused by the new King's desire to marry a divorced woman.

League of Nations Union conference at Eastbourne.
Viscount Cecil, centre, in black hat, with Joan immediately behind him
and Leslie four along to his right.

One of Leslie's jobs on arriving for the conference had been to collect the president of the League, Viscount Cecil of Chelwood, from his home near Haywards Heath, about 30 miles from Eastbourne. [21] On arriving at Chelwood Gate Leslie had been alarmed to see that the area in front of the Viscount's house was packed with sharp stones, and having managed to walk carefully to the front door and asked how he could drive in to collect his charge, the footman informed him that he couldn't, since his lordship didn't like motorists, but was happy to walk to the car. The next challenge was fitting the tall, long-legged Viscount into Leslie's small Austin 10, and when they finally arrived at the conference, the Viscount complimented his chauffeur on his driving, telling him that although he was an ardent anti-motorist and avoided cars at all costs, it had been the best drive he had ever experienced. Incidentally, Viscount Cecil was a speaker of Esperanto, and had proposed in 1921 that the League of Nations adopt it as the solution to the language problem; it's quite probable that Leslie's decision to learn Esperanto later on was influenced by his association with Lord Cecil.

A few months after the conference, Leslie and Joan had another distinguished passenger in the Austin 10, Bishop Blunt, who soon after travelling with them was instrumental in the abdication of Edward VIII, sparked by his address to the Diocesan Conference and his concern about King Edward's casual attitude towards religion; during the journey with Leslie and Joan from North London to the West End the Bishop's hat was blown out of the car, Joan leaping out in order to retrieve it.

Joan and her parents took their annual holiday in August, and 1936 was to be no exception. During the 1930s it was the custom for the major railway companies to take old carriages out of service, convert them into what they called 'camping coach' holiday homes, and then let them out to holiday-makers at quiet rural stations close to walking country or the seaside. Seemingly Joan's parents had planned what Leslie referred to as a 'coach holiday' that year, and although he doesn't specify the nature of their holiday, it's more than likely that it would have been the camping coach variety. However, Leslie had other ideas, and when he offered to take them on a two-week tour of some of England's lovely countryside in his car, they changed their plans, possibly due to the fact that motoring was still a novelty and the era of the motorway was still a long way off. Thankfully Joan kept a daily diary of her holiday, with detailed accounts of where they went, and giving a glimpse not only of her delight in experiencing new towns and countryside, but also of her blossoming relationship with Leslie.

Joan with her parents on Lake Derwentwater, summer 1936.

The holiday-makers left North London on August 8th, calling into Oxford for lunch, Stratford-upon-Avon for afternoon tea, and spending the night at the Lord Leycester Hotel in Warwick. When they drove through Bourton-on-the-Water the following day Joan noted in her diary that they were very amused to see that the dentist there was called Gore Boodle; and then it was on to Worcester, arriving just in time to attend Evensong at the cathedral before driving on to a guest house in the Forest of Dean. There is no reference in Joan's journal to how her parents related to their daughter and her 'older' admirer, although she did note that "the atmosphere is clearing, we are all getting more friendly," at the end of the second day. The following day they visited Tintern Abbey, Monmouth Castle and Hereford Cathedral, spending the night in Church Stretton where Joan noted that they "walked in the evening. Getting on well and having a fine time."

Although Leslie had been as far north as Windermere during visits to his sister and family, the north of England was new territory for Joan and her parents, and as they left the familiar south behind them, Joan's diary listed the towns they passed on their way --- Shrewsbury, Wrexham, Chester, Birkenhead, and then the Mersey tunnel, which she found "very thrilling", before driving through the city of Liverpool where she was "very amused at the women wearing shawls". Their destination that night was Barrow-in-Furness, where Leslie's sister, Elsie, lived with her family, and if this was Joan's first encounter with them, she doesn't mention it, although she does comment on the two "sweet" children, Eileen and Shirley. Rooms had been reserved in the Victoria Hotel, but when Stanley was taken ill during the evening, it was decided that he should be taken care of in Elsie's home. Thankfully his illness was short-lived, and after breakfast the next morning the party were able to drive north towards the Lake District, visiting Ruskin's home at Brantwood and staying at the Waterhead Hotel overlooking Lake Coniston. It was Leslie's turn to be unwell, although he, too, recovered quickly, and after breakfast they set off again, passing Little and Great Langdale, and arriving in Ambleside in time for lunch. Having visited Wordsworth's home in Hawkshead during the afternoon they spent the night at a hotel in Newby Bridge, where the waiter turned off the lights, plunging Joan and Leslie into darkness as they sat together on the verandah.

The holidaymakers continued for another week, following an exhausting routine of driving, sightseeing and walking, taking in Grasmere, Keswick, Ennerdale, Wastwater, clocking up the miles in the Austin10, pushing it to its limits up the Kirkstone Pass, and no doubt enjoying the opportunity to spend time together in such magnificent countryside.

By the time the holiday was over Leslie was even more sure that Joan was the girl he must marry. However, she was only sixteen and was still living at home with her parents, whilst Leslie, on the other hand, was nearing his thirties, and was running a well-established dental practice in North London. The idea of marriage surely worried both sets of parents as well as other relatives and friends, but despite all apparent obstacles, they were given permission to become engaged on Joan's 17th birthday, March 17th, 1937.

Chapter Eleven

The Linden drama

During the early months of Leslie's engagement to Joan, his Linden cousins, Eva and Ivy, became embroiled in what was to become a dramatic international incident. Not much is known of the Linden fortunes during the preceding years, and it is to be presumed that their parents, Charles and Florrie, were still trying to make ends meet as musicians and music-hall artists. By 1937 it's quite probable that Ivy and Eva were no longer in the Ivy Benson women's jazz band, although they were still active as musicians, often appearing together as the Linden sisters.

It was while Eva was working in Berlin in the early 1920s that she met and married a Russian band leader and singer by the name of Rheinhard Lowenburg, who had become a naturalised German Jew. Soon after they moved to London in the mid-thirties with their young daughter, the marriage broke down, and Rheinhard, known to family and colleagues as Sacha, returned to Russia. From this point onwards details are scant and cloaked in mystery, but some time during 1936 Eva received a letter from Russia, written by a woman who claimed to be living with Sasha; her name was Zina, and keen to clarify the situation, Eva dropped everything and travelled to Russia, where, on arrival in Leningrad she discovered that Sacha and his lady friend were living two days' travel away. Since Eva had a pressing engagement waiting in London, she abandoned her quest and returned home. But her return was short-lived; she was keen to put her relationship with Sacha behind her, and in order to divorce him she obviously believed that confronting him in Russia was the best solution, regardless of the current political situation in the country.

Russia had undergone a revolution, and was in the grip of Stalin's Great Purge at the time Eva was planning her trip. Anybody Stalin considered to be a danger to his policies, or who appeared to have a will of their own, was sent to labour camps, known as the 'gulag', in far off Siberia; of the twenty million who arrived there, at least half died. No-one trusted anyone else in a climate of blame and fear, and people disappeared from their homes in the middle of the night, often never to be seen or heard of again. Ethnic groups were persecuted, and religion, which was considered to be the 'opiate of the people', was forbidden. This was the Russia which Eva planned to visit in order to divorce her husband, and without further thought she arranged to undertake a four month concert tour with her sister, leaving her ten-year-old daughter in the care of relatives at home.

The tour began in December 1936, and with the divorce safely under her belt by March 1937, Eva proceeded to marry her young interpreter, Sabarovski, on April 14th. No other information is available as to how she managed the concerts, how she and Ivy travelled from place to place in a Russia which was rife with danger, or why she made the decision to marry so soon after her divorce. There is no information, either, on why Eva and Ivy then travelled to Leningrad in order to take the boat home to England, or why Eva's new husband wasn't with them; all Eva stated much later was that since the Russians had confiscated their passports, they were unable to sail, and had to share a room at the Astoria hotel for the night. During the early hours of the morning two men from OGPU [22] (political police) accompanied by the assistant manager of the hotel walked into the sisters' bedroom, ransacked and confiscated their papers, and forced them to keep silent until, about four hours later, Eva was taken away and charged with espionage and terrorism, Ivy being advised to leave Russia as soon as possible. According to Ivy's interview with the Express newspaper on reaching England, Rheinhard Lowenburg and Zina had also been arrested in another Leningrad hotel during the same night.

Eva, Ivy and Hugo Linden, (Leslie's cousins).
Hugo worked with the best orchestras in London as a viola player.

Months of silence followed; to all intents and purposes Eva had disappeared, and the family waiting earnestly in England felt completely powerless to seek her whereabouts or find a solution to bringing her home from Russia. It was at this juncture that Leslie decided to use his involvement with the League of Nations Union in order to move the disquieting situation forward, and soon after he contacted the foreign secretary, Anthony Eden, Eva was freed from her Russian prison and able to travel back to London.

It was on Eva's return that the press eagerly took up her story, giving a glimpse of what she had experienced during her imprisonment. The Daily Express printed several short articles during the early months of 1938, quoting her various comments but leaving a great deal to the imagination:

"I found the mattress too bumpy for my liking, so I asked the wardress to give me another. Then I asked for a carpet to cover the floor. But that was too much. I don't remember how many cross-examinations I had, but it must have been about twenty, lasting three to four hours each. They told me I could go home the minute I had confessed everything. 'You know your husband is a Trotskyist,' they told me. 'What exactly is a Trotskyist?' I asked them. 'You know he has been conspiring against the State,' they'd reply. 'How has he been doing that,' I would ask? 'Now, admit he's an enemy of the Soviet Union,' they'd plead. And so it would go on for hours. They never got any further. I was cross-examined, sometimes by one, at other times by two or three young officials, all looking very smart in elegantly cut suits.

The young fellows were very sweet and polite about trying to get me into signing a 'mad' confession of things I'd never done. I refused to sign: I know that would have been my own death warrant. The foxtrot and tangos I composed puzzled the OGPU boys. They thought it was some kind of cypher and that I must be a master spy --- I kept on reminding them that I was a British subject and that if they ill-treated me there would be trouble. I think that kept me safe. I composed waltzes and fox-trots in jail to pass the time. But I'm free now."

The Daily Express commented that "While in Russia Eva divorced her German husband, and two days before her arrest, married a young Russian. Both men, it is believed, were arrested on the same night as the sisters. Only news of them since was a rumour that the Russian had been released. The delay in securing Eva's freedom was caused, it is stated, by difficulties in establishing her nationality after her two marriages. She is expected home on Sunday and her mother, Mrs. Linden, of Mount Pleasant Lane, Hackney, E, is now preparing a grand home-coming party."

The story seemingly ends on Eva's return, and there is no record of how her life proceeded from then on. Her Russian husband was never seen or heard of again, and it's tempting to wonder if, indeed, both her husbands ended their lives in the gulags of Siberia.

Chapter Twelve

The engagement, a threat of war, and a wedding

Marriage was on the horizon for Leslie and Joan, and the future was full of promise. Joan was everything Leslie had ever wanted in a wife, and her acceptance of his hand in marriage showed that she loved him too. During their long engagement they spent many hours playing cello and piano duets together, and when Leslie asked Joan to choose a cello sonata for their entry in the London Festival, Leslie's teacher at Trinity College was horrified to learn that she had chosen the rather difficult Beethoven A Major, which was beyond Leslie's capacity as a cellist, but not Joan's as a pianist. Unfortunately there is no record of how successful they were, although Leslie was no doubt encouraged by his young fiance's enthusiasm, for a little while later he passed the Trinity Grade 8 cello examination. He was also keen to help Joan in her own musical endeavours, and when he arranged for her to have violin and singing lessons, she was happy to accept.

It was during their engagement that Leslie came to realise that his dream-girl was more than capable of putting forward her personal opinions, and that there were times when he found it difficult to consult with her on matters of importance. Dorothy had disciplined her daughter rigidly, so rigidly in fact that Joan had already decided that should she have children of her own, she would bring them up quite differently. It's possible that in becoming engaged to Leslie at

18, Joan discovered the delights of having her own opinions and the freedom to share them; for share them she did, and at times the relationship with Leslie was tested to its limits. For whatever reason, Joan accepted a date with another man during her engagement to Leslie, who was so angry that he chased her round the dining room table. It didn't bode well for their future marriage, but as luck would have it, help did come a little later, and in a form which both Leslie and Joan later agreed was the saving of them as a couple.

In the meantime, the engagement continued on a fairly even keel. During the summer of 1937 they holidayed in Lynmouth, North Devon, with Dorothy and Stanley chaperoning, and a year later in Criccieth, on the edge of Snowdonia. Unfortunately Joan was taken ill with a severe throat infection, being prescribed M and B 693 (sulphapyridine), which was a very early form of antibiotic before the general use of penicillin several years later. Since Joan was laid low, Leslie and Stanley bravely decided to tackle mount Snowdon, taking it stage by stage until they eventually reached the summit; this was a real achievement for Leslie with his health history, and it was only after several years that he admitted to Stanley that he had persevered in order to give his future father-in-law a good impression, Stanley admitting that he had kept going for exactly the same reason!

It was while they were in Criccieth that the crisis in Europe deepened, the possibility of war ever more menacing as Hitler threatened to invade more and more countries. Living in Criccieth at that time was the famous and elderly statesman David Lloyd George, who had been Prime Minister from 1916 until 1922, and since he was giving a speech during their visit, Joan and Leslie decided to attend. The theme was, 'Is it peace or war?', a question which everyone was asking themselves as the situation deteriorated. Indeed, the current Prime Minister, Neville Chamberlain, spent September 1938 consulting with Hitler in a desperate attempt to avoid war, and after three visits to Germany and some complicated negotiations, he returned from his final visit on September 29th in triumph, believing that in signing an agreement he had managed to avert war. The King and the populace were overjoyed, little realising that Hitler had no intention of honouring the agreement.

The following months were tense, for although people were still hopeful of a peaceful outcome, serious preparations were being made for possible air-raids; there were plans for the evacuation of women and children, city parks were dug up in order to provide air-raid shelters, and gas masks were distributed. Joan's letters to Leslie at this time offer glimpses into the personal lives of people as they fearfully watched hopes of peace crumble around them; "The world has gone mad," she wrote in one letter, as she reported the mass exodus from her home street, people leaving for Oxford, Gloucester, and various places in Buckinghamshire; "I still haven't got my gas mask," she continued, "I really don't see that they will be of much use, all the same I shall get one - just in case. --- Regent's Park is being knocked about a bit, the trees are being chopped down, and there are guns all over the place as well as men in khaki and tents and things. Finsbury Park is being dug into trenches."

It was in this heightened national state of anticipation and fear that Leslie and Joan prepared for their
wedding in July 1939, planning their future and looking
for a house of their own. Since thousands of people who
were in a position to do so were leaving London due to the
threat of war, there were more than enough houses for Leslie
and Joan to choose from, and at very reasonable prices.
Having visited a few houses, they decided to settle on one
in Southgate, North London; number 19 Wynchgate seemed
the perfect location, conveniently situated just a short walk
from the Underground Station, and having a lovely peaceful
back garden. The house had a large lounge, a breakfast
room, four bedrooms, and a garage, and as Leslie and Joan
watched their home take shape with decorating and brand
new furniture, the future certainly looked promising, with
the beautiful Ibach Concert Grand piano which Leslie gave
to Joan as a wedding present setting the scene for a life filled
with music. Leslie took out a large loan from a building
society in order to purchase the new house at a cost of
£1,500, but as the young couple approached their marriage
and the prospect of a lovely home, all the effort and expense
seemed worth while. Joan took her responsibilities as a
home maker very seriously, budgeting and planning everything down to the last penny; she filled a notebook with
requirements and costs, listing each room separately, and
including in her list, "umbrella stand, one pound and four
shillings; two elbow chairs; Monks bench, six pounds and
five shillings; [23] Wireless set, ten pounds; Kerb suite, three

pounds; Mirror and hooks, two pounds and eight shillings; Bedstead, twenty-five pounds; Table (oak), eighteen pounds; Sideboard, eighteen pounds and ten shillings ---".

Despite living fairly close to one another and seeing each other regularly, letters passed between Leslie and Joan almost daily, and by this time they were addressing each other as "Micky" and "Bunny", with Micky being Joan and Bunny, Leslie. As time went on other endearments crept in, such as "My dearest Bunny-boy" and "beloved sweetheart", and all the while Leslie was working longer and longer hours in the surgery, often well into the evenings, and always on a Saturday morning. It was an exacting schedule, and with preparations for the wedding taking place in an atmosphere of constant worry concerning the strengthening threat of war, Leslie often suffered from exhaustion.

Despite the hard work and apprehension Leslie and Joan were able to focus most of their attention on their future together, and were married on July 22nd 1939, in St Stephen's Church, Bush Hill Park. Following the reception in the church hall they were whisked off to Dunsmure Road, and after a grand welcome to the very new Mr. and Mrs. Sparey by Betty, the maid, they set off for their honeymoon in Leslie's Austin 10. Having spent the first night in Tring, they began moving slowly north, stopping off at Stamford, York and Carlisle, and making a quick trip over the Scottish Border before settling for a few days in the Lake District. In Keswick they stayed in a small hotel overlooking the mountains beyond Lake Derwentwater, and although it was July and supposedly the holiday season, they had great

The Wedding.

difficulty in finding a cafe or restaurant which remained open during the evening. On leaving Keswick the following morning they drove past the dental surgery in Station Road, and when Joan expressed a wish that Leslie set up his practice in just such a place, his response was that maybe when he retired in thirty years they could consider living somewhere like Keswick. Little did either of them dream that Leslie's passing comment would prove to be true far sooner than they expected. Leaving Keswick behind and heading south they spent some time in Grasmere before continuing the long journey back to London, and by the time they reached home the worsening political situation across Europe was on everybody's mind.

The Spareys on their honeymoon in the Lake District.

The Spareys planned to spend a week or so at 24, Dunsmure Road before moving into their new home in Wynchgate; but the move didn't happen. Leslie's memoirs are frustratingly sketchy regarding developments at this time, but it's safe to assume that all his energy was focused on the dental practice, which was still in the Dunsmure Road house, and which continued to occupy most of his time. Arrangements were made for his parents to stay with distant relatives for a while in Yeovil, but little did they realise as they left Dunsmure Road that it was the last time they would set foot in the house that they had occupied for over thirty years.

Chapter Thirteen

Outbreak of war

On September 1st 1939, Germany began its invasion of Poland, and as the prospect of war loomed ever closer, plans for the evacuation of children and pregnant mothers from London and other vulnerable areas were instigated. On the same day, blackout regulations were imposed, all windows and doors to be covered with thick curtains or other suitable materials so that no light at all could be visible from outside. Air-raid wardens were appointed in order to make sure that regulations were observed, and part of their duty was to call at houses which were showing light, issuing the occupants with a stern warning. Street lights were either switched off or deflected downwards, as were traffic lights and vehicle headlights, causing many fatal accidents on the roads.

War was declared at 11am on Sunday September 3rd. Leslie and Joan sat quietly by their wireless as the Prime Minister spoke, and just a few minutes later the air-raid siren sounded; Leslie and Joan ran for their new shelter down in the cellar, but it was a false alarm. As well as the cellar, they had had an Anderson shelter installed at the bottom of the garden, a semi-circular metal construction which they had furnished sparingly with chairs, rugs, emergency lights and rations. Concerning that first morning at the outbreak of World War II Leslie later wrote, "it was a very odd feeling on that Sunday morning, and I'll never forget the contrast between the glorious September sunshine and the unbelievable thought that we were actually at war and that injury and death could come at any moment."

Although during the first few months after the declaration of war nothing appeared to change much for those living in England, Scotland was subjected to several attacks from the Germans, most notably in October 1939 at Scapa Flow, off the island of Orkney, when HMS Royal Oak was sunk with eight hundred and thirty-three lives lost, and at Rosyth, when the German Luftwaffe began bombing British warships. The initial nine months of the war became known as the phoney war, since during that period there were no major military operations by the Western Allies against the German Reich. Most action during the phoney war took place at sea, as German U-boats and warships, joined later by Italian submarines, struggled to stop the Allied convoys from transporting military equipment and supplies across the Atlantic to Great Britain and the Soviet Union, a struggle which lasted throughout the whole six years of the war.

Before the war Britain was importing about fifty-five million tons of food each year from abroad, but when German submarines began attacking British supply ships after the start of the war, the Government brought in a system of rationing in order to guarantee that the population received an equal amount of food each week. Each person was supplied with a ration book which enabled him to purchase food in shops of his choice, the shopkeepers making sure that they had enough food for their registered customers; already by early January 1940 sugar, butter and bacon were rationed, with more items being added as time went on. People began growing their own vegetables, and in October 1939 the 'Dig for Victory' campaign encouraged as many people as possible to keep an allotment, whilst lawns and flower beds were converted into vegetable gardens. Bananas and lemons soon disappeared altogether, and oranges were reserved for children and pregnant women. Rationing of food, petrol and clothes became a way of life in Britain, and although some restrictions were lifted soon after the war, it wasn't until July 1954 that it was finally put to rest.

These were the conditions to which Leslie and Joan were accustomising themselves as they launched themselves into married life. They were still living in the house in Dunsmure Road, possibly because the blackout and dangerous driving conditions at night made it too difficult for Leslie to travel the 6 miles to their own home in Wynchgate after his long day's work in the surgery. By this time Herbert and Amy had moved from Yeovil into a boarding house in Rickmansworth which Leslie and Joan had found for them after several weekends of search; although no explanation is given, it's quite possible that the reason for not returning to their home in Dunsmure Road was Amy's failing health, particularly her poor eyesight, which made living in a house with stairs too difficult and unsafe. In many ways daily life carried on as usual, with the dental practice as busy as ever, and Joan settling into her new role as a housewife.

At the beginning of 1940 Leslie was elected as secretary of the senior branch of the League of Nations Union. As a couple Leslie and Joan began thinking about how they could best help their young friends through the long dark evenings of the blackout, and they started hosting a series of fortnightly discussion meetings in their home. Each meeting was facilitated by a guest speaker, with topics such as, 'How to end the war', 'Communism', and 'Federal Union', and it was when no speaker was planned that Joan suggested asking someone from the Oxford Group. Leslie already knew about the Oxford Group, which was a Christian organisation founded by American Christian missionary Dr. Frank Buchman, his philosophy being that the root of all problems, whether between individuals or nations, was the personal problem of selfishness, which could only be overcome through surrendering to the will to God, and that this could be accomplished by daily reflection, prayer, and 'listening' to God's guidance. Since Joan had declared herself to be an agnostic, Leslie was delighted that she was willing to consider a speaker from what was in essence a Christian organisation, and he lost no time in booking one. To Joan's consternation, not one, but six speakers turned up, and she didn't enjoy the evening at all, especially when they offered to help her in the kitchen. But Leslie was obviously very keen on what he felt these new acquaintances had to offer, and promptly invited them back two weeks later.

What Leslie and Joan experienced through the philosophy of the Oxford Group was to become the foundation of a long successful marriage. Their relationship had already suffered serious disunity during the engagement, and there had been times when Leslie, particularly, had been seriously concerned for their future as a couple. Joan was young and headstrong, and she wasn't used to consultation. Already in their new marriage there were arguments, and Leslie felt powerless to find a solution. But the Oxford group, with its teachings on reconciliation and forgiveness, offered the solution they both believed they needed at the time, with its focus on not 'who' is right but 'what' is right, and a daily life based on the principals of four absolute standards, 'honesty', 'purity', 'unselfishness' and 'love'. As they began to experience a daily time of reflection and put into practice the principles which the Group advocated, Leslie and Joan believed that they had found a blueprint for successful marriage.

By the time Leslie and Joan were involved in the Oxford Group it had been relaunched as Moral Re-Armament (MRA), as the result of a statement which its founder, Frank Buchman, had made in front of three thousand people in East Ham Town Hall, London, on 29th May 1938. "The crisis is fundamentally a moral one," he had said. "The nations must re-arm morally. Moral recovery is essentially the forerunner of economic recovery. Moral recovery creates not crisis but confidence and unity in every phase of life." [24] Believing that they had discovered not only the answer to their own problems, but also to those threatening the future safety of the world, the Spareys threw themselves whole-heartedly into local activities. Regular meetings continued in their home, and having read a newly published book entitled Unser Kampf (Our Struggle) [25] by the Liberal MP Sir Richard Acland, Leslie wrote to the author in order to ask for a speaker on the subject; Sir Richard responded by sending his aunt, a Miss Cropper, and although Leslie doesn't specify the link in his memoirs, it's probable that Miss Cropper was connected with MRA. (For information on MRA see *Appendix 2*)

The phoney war came to an end on May 10th 1940, as German troops marched into Belgium, The Netherlands and Luxembourg; on the same day the British Prime Minister, Neville Chamberlain, resigned his position, to be succeeded by Winston Churchill and a newly appointed coalition Government. For the ordinary citizen living in Britain a new and extremely rigid regime now controlled every aspect of daily life. During the phoney war thirty-five percent of evacuated London schoolchildren had returned home, but between May and June 1940 a further one hundred and sixty thousand children were evacuated from strategic coastal areas, followed by another sixty thousand over the following year. The 'blackout' had already been operating since September 1939, and by the summer of 1940 all street signs, signposts and maps had been removed in order to confuse the invaders, no doubt confusing the population at the same time.

During the First World War France, Germany, Italy, and Britain had used barrage balloons; as part of the Royal Air Force, 'Balloon Command' had been established in 1938 in order to protect vulnerable targets from enemy dive bombers, including ports, industrial sites, and cities. By mid-1940, one thousand four hundred balloons were already in operation, a third of them over the London area. In essence, they were large balloons held down by metal cables and used to avoid aircraft attack by damaging the aircraft as they collided with the cables, also making the attacker's approach more difficult. People were able to decide by the position of the barrage balloons whether or not it was safe to be out on the streets; if they were down, it was a clear indication that all was safe, and if they were up, that danger was imminent. The terrifying sound of the wailing air raid sirens sent people running for cover, some in their shelters and many in the London Underground stations, and only when the siren gave the all-clear were they able to emerge.

Life continued much as before for Leslie and Joan, since instructions were that young dental surgeons should not volunteer for the dental services of the armed forces, but wait for the automatic call-up. Leslie decided to offer his services to the civil defence, and on hearing that dentists would be required to act as emergency anaesthetists in First-Aid Posts, he attended a special post-graduate course for doctors and dentists at the Royal Northern Hospital, as well as a refresher course in First Aid.

Fear of bombing and the nightly blackouts were a constant worry, and the plight of domestic pets no doubt added to the distress, especially since Leslie and Joan had the extremely unpleasant task one Sunday morning of driving over to The Meadway in Bush Hill Park, collecting as many cats as possible, and taking them to be destroyed. This policy had commenced right at the beginning of the war as a result of the forming of the National Air Raid Precautions Animals Committee (NARPAC), which advised pet owners that if they couldn't guarantee safety of their pets they should have them humanely destroyed. The cull began soon after war was declared in September 1939, with as many as seven hundred and fifty thousand animals being killed in one week; reasons for this policy included the fact that there were no food rations for pets, and a fear that as the bombing intensified hundreds of stray animals would be left roaming the streets. In an already distressing atmosphere of dread as the war progressed, this policy no doubt broke the hearts of thousands of families, particularly in urban areas.

In 1940 the Minister of Aircraft Production, Lord Beaverbrook, called on the people of Great Britain to help him in producing more fighter aircraft, urging them to donate their aluminium pans in order to transform them into Wellingtons, Spitfires and Hurricanes; Leslie noted in his memoirs that in Dunsmure Road there was a house-to-house collection of aluminium kitchen-ware, and although on that occasion number 24 didn't donate, such was the national response that great mountains of pots and pans, totalling over seventy thousand tons of aluminium, appeared all over the UK. It was during the same period that on returning home after a weekend away, Leslie and Joan found that all their wrought-iron decorative railings had been sawn off and taken, as had been all the iron work in the road; at that time the authorities were also requisitioning many of the 19th century iron railings and gates surrounding cemeteries, parks and squares in Britain's towns and cities. Rumours later abounded as to what actually happened to all the iron that had been collected; one theory held to the belief that since it was unsuitable for manufacturing aircraft it had been either dropped in the Thames estuary or buried in quarries, another firmly believing that it had been recycled and turned into planes, but since there are no surviving records to support either view, the question remains unanswered.

The first few months of the the new year brought with them severe tests for Leslie and Joan as they set about dealing with the mounting difficulties brought on by the war. Their maid, Betty, still living in the family home at Dunsmure Road, underwent an operation for a gastric ulcer, and needed careful nursing during her convalescence; her strict diet was obviously something which she struggled with and one of Joan's chores was to keep Betty out of the kitchen and away from forbidden foods. A little while later a married couple who were close friends of the Sparey's became so ill that they were unable to take care of themselves, Joan offering to take them in and nurse them herself.

In order to ease the tension, Leslie and Joan began attending the City Temple in Holborn, where they enjoyed listening to the talks of Methodist Minister, Dr. Leslie Weatherhead, whom they knew through his connection with Moral Re-Armament. Such was the popularity of his talks that people travelled from all over London to hear him, often queuing for hours in order to guarantee a seat. Despite his popularity, he was considered by more conservative Christians to be a highly controversial figure due to his questioning of some of the central mores of the Christian faith, and for his inclusion in it of some aspects from other religions and spiritualism. Leslie found him to be compassionate, sympathetic, and at times rather sentimental, whilst appreciating his sense of humour and a deep understanding of human nature; through their common link with Moral Re-Armament Leslie and Joan no doubt met Weatherhead occasionally at a personal level, and without specifying exactly why, Leslie noted in his memoirs that he was extremely grateful for his help and inspiration.

Many of Leslie's dental patients at this time were Jewish refugees who had fled from Germany and Austria, and some of them became good friends. He particularly remembered a gentleman who invited both Leslie and Joan to visit him in his bed-sitter nearby, where he told them about some of the terrible ordeals to which he and his fellow Jews had been subjected in Germany before escaping to London. Soon after the visit Leslie began making him a set of dentures since he had only a few teeth left of his own, but before they were ready, Leslie saw, to his horror, his patient being marched up the road under arrest; along with thousands of others, he was being transported to an internment camp on the Isle of Man. After some enquiries and formalities, Leslie was able to send the half-finished dentures to a dentist on the island who no doubt finished the job and delivered them accordingly.

As the summer of 1940 advanced, bombing over Britain began with daylight raids at the beginning of July, two months before the start of the Blitz. Wick aerodrome, in the north of Scotland, was the first to be hit, followed by industrial sites in Norwich, with many towns along the south coast being targeted as part of the Luftwaffe's Operation Sealion. Finally, on August 24th, Central London received its first hit, intended for military sites on the outskirts, but damaging the medieval church of St. Giles, Cripplegate which had miraculously survived the Great Fire of 1666; several houses were also destroyed in the hit, with a resulting loss of life. The outrage that followed led the Prime Minister to order the bombing of Berlin the following night. On September 7th Hitler gave orders that bombing be focused on London instead of strategic airfields and bases, and on the same night three hundred and forty-eight bombers, escorted by six hundred and seventeen fighters, hit London.

In the build-up to the bombing of London on August 24th, Leslie's health had begun to deteriorate, with severe weight loss, lack of sleep, and heart trouble in the form of rhythmic irregularity. Hiding in the cellar during that first night of London bombing, Leslie and Joan made the decision to leave London for a while in the hope that it would give him the opportunity to recuperate. Early the following morning they packed up as many belongings as they could manage in the few suitcases they had, using a large travelling rug tied with string for the patient record cards, the gas masks, and other bits and pieces. Too ill to collect his car from the garage some distance away, Leslie ordered a taxi to take them to Paddington Station; little did they realise, as they left 24 Dunsmure Road, that they were leaving for the last time, and that life as they knew it would never be the same again.

Chapter Fourteen

The refugees

It's not clear whether Leslie and Joan had made any plans regarding where they would flee to when they left their home, but when they arrived at Paddington Station they took the first train to Oxford, where they managed to find a cheap boarding house for the night; any hope for a peaceful few hours, however, was dashed by the constant drone of planes flying overhead. Thankfully they were able to contact friends who lived in Powick, near Worcester, a dentist and his wife whom they had met through the Oxford Group, and who invited them to stay in their home for a few nights. The plan was to stay in the area for a couple of weeks so that Leslie could recuperate before returning home, and with this in mind they booked themselves into a guest house in Worcester; but no sooner had they settled in than Leslie's condition deteriorated dramatically. This was certainly a challenge for Joan. She was twenty-one years of age, had led a protected life, and wasn't used to managing a critical situation without the advice of her close family back in London; however, she more than proved herself capable, quickly sending for a doctor who was able to prescribe some medication to ease Leslie's physical symptoms. It was then a matter of waiting for the medicine to take effect, and Joan used the time to go through the dental record cards of all Leslie's current patients, writing to all one hundred of them in order to tell them that he was ill, and that she would let them know when their dental treatment could be resumed.

Any hope for a quiet interlude were very quickly dashed when bombing raids began over Birmingham, about twenty-five miles from Worcester, and since there appeared to be no improvement in Leslie's condition the decision was made to move as far away as they possibly could from the danger zone. Remembering their visits to the Lake District, Joan and Leslie decided to head north for Keswick, despite the fact that they knew no-one there. Since Leslie was still weak it was probably Joan who bought a guide book and made the telephone booking at a small hotel in Keswick, and as soon as they could the Spareys set off by train, changing at Birmingham, where in the station broken glass and debris was being cleared up from the previous night's bombing raid.

Thankfully Keswick proved to be the refuge which Leslie so badly needed; Fletcher's Hotel in St John's Street stood right opposite the church, and despite the fact that the clock struck every quarter of an hour, Leslie managed to sleep through the night for the first time in weeks.

Having escaped from London and abandoned the dental practice, the question of income soon became a priority. Thankfully Leslie had taken out sickness insurance which brought in about £8 per week, but with full board at Fletchers hotel being between £4 to £5 a week, there was little margin for anything extra, Leslie reluctantly needing to draw on his savings.

As soon as they arrived in Keswick he set about locating a good, reliable doctor; the National Health Service was still a pipe-dream in 1940, and medical care wouldn't become a free commodity until after the war, but no doubt Leslie's insurance covered his costs while he was ill. Having undergone a series of medical tests, it became clear that Leslie wouldn't be in a condition to return to London for some time, and as a result finding cheaper accommodation became a matter of urgency.

In the years leading up to the war Keswick had already established itself as the main centre for tourism in Cumberland and Westmorland, being labelled as 'The capital of the Lake District' in an article written in 'The Manchester Guardian' in 1934. [26] At the outbreak of the Second World War it had become a safe haven for Jewish refugees and evacuees, with available accommodation at a premium, making it extremely difficult for newcomers to find suitable rooms. Thankfully Leslie and Joan managed to find a boarding house at number 5, Borrowdale Road, where they were able to stay for several months. Decades later Leslie's memory served him well as he recorded one or two unforgettable moments in his memoirs of the time he and Joan spent at the house in Borrowdale Road: "It was rough and ready but homely, and we shared the sitting room with others - a rather posh lady who suffered very badly from migraine, for whom I had to inject when she was almost prostrate, and a middle aged man who developed pneumonia; Joan and I were delegated by the doctor to attend to him during the night, and on one occasion he became delirious and fought with us! I was very thin and had lost a lot of weight, and we heard later that people felt so sorry for the young wife whose husband seemed to have 'one leg in the grave.'"

It was during their stay in Borrowdale Road that Leslie and Joan received a phone call from her father in London, bearing devastating news; during a German raid on October 9th 1940, a bomb had fallen on Dunsmure Road, and their home had been badly damaged. Stanley had bravely visited the scene as soon as he could after the bombing, by which time looters had already taken a few household items; however, the dental equipment and some of the furniture was intact, and arrangements were made to transfer as much as possible to the new house in Southgate, where it remained for some months until somewhere suitable could be found to store it in Keswick.

Despite the trauma of the bombing at Dunsmure Road, life for Leslie and Joan gradually improved as Leslie's severe symptoms showed signs of subsiding, and since he was unfit to serve with the Royal Army Dental Corps his doctor suggested that he could do a little dental surgery locally, especially since the two Keswick dentists, only one of whom was qualified, were overwhelmed with patients and were struggling to cope. After some negotiation with Mr. Gregg, the qualified dentist, Leslie was taken on as his assistant for £8 per week. The surgery he found himself working in was quite primitive compared to what he had been used to in his London practice, and he was particularly amused by the extremely old dental chair which was cranked up and down with a removable handle. Physical limitations aside, he began to feel very much at home both in his surgery and with his patients, and although his employer had a reputation for being difficult, they formed a good relationship. Three times married, Mr. Gregg had finally found happiness with his young housekeeper, who bore him twins, and he spent his leisure hours learning to play the flute and growing tomatoes; sadly he died within a year of his retirement.

As Leslie settled into his dental work, Joan volunteered some of her time to the Women's Voluntary Service, which played a key part in the war effort, particularly helping in the evacuation of civilians from urban areas and organising the complicated job of food rationing; in Keswick the main focus of the Service was on the care of foreign refugees, who had stretched the normal population of the town from four or five thousand to an estimated twenty thousand. Joan was also offered some music teaching, including a small group of young children playing percussion instruments; but her main commitment was to teaching piano at the Methodist-run Hunmanby Gap Girls School, the Middle and Junior departments of which had been evacuated to Armathwaite Hall and Bassen Fell, just north of Bassenthwaite Lake, near Keswick. Hunmanby Gap wasn't the only school to evacuate to Keswick; Roedean Independent Boarding School for Girls had relocated from their clifftop premises on the south coast of England to the Keswick Hotel, classroom space spilling out into the hotel garage, the Methodist Church Rooms and parts of the adjacent Keswick railway station, including the waiting room, which was still being used by waiting passengers. Students from the Liverpool Orphanage, Newcastle High School, and St. Katherine's College, Liverpool, also spent the war years in Keswick.

Most of the foreign refugees who found themselves in Keswick were Jews escaping from Nazi Germany, and amongst them was a couple whom Leslie and Joan had met in London not long before the bombing had begun. Julius Katay and his wife had arrived in London from Vienna, where Julius had been the conductor at the Merchants' Singing Academy, as well as assistant to the great Bruno Walter, who had conducted the Vienna Philharmonic Orchestra between 1933 and 1938. The Katay's escape from the Nazis was miraculous enough, but their escape during a bombing raid in London was probably more extraordinary still. One evening as they were entertaining guests there was a bombing raid, and as their guests ran for shelter under the grand piano, Julius and his wife suddenly remembered that their kitten hadn't been fed, and ran upstairs in order to find it. Unfortunately their house suffered a direct hit, burying them in the falling rubble; when eventually they were rescued by a fireman the kitten jumped onto Mrs. Katay's shoulder as they were being carried down the ladder; had it not been for the kitten they would certainly have been under the piano with their guests, none of whom survived. How long the Katays stayed in Keswick isn't recorded, but some time after the war ended they moved to Christchurch in Hampshire, where Julius died in September 1957.

Unfortunately Leslie's memoirs don't give the reason why he and Joan left the boarding house in Borrowdale Road, simply stating that they moved into two tiny rooms in St. Herbert's Street, a move which wasn't at all convenient. The bathroom and kitchen were situated on the other side of the landlady's sitting room, which meant that they were required to knock on her door any time they needed access; to make matters even more uncomfortable, there was no lighting or heating in their bedroom, and one very cold morning Leslie discovered that his dentures had frozen solid in a glass of ice!

Joan with her parents outside the rented house in Herbert Street, Keswick.

It was during this period that Leslie's parents, Herbert and Amy, moved north from Rickmansworth, taking two rooms in a house in Eskin Street, not far from Leslie and Joan. Furniture and some dental equipment arrived from the house in Southgate at around the same time, Leslie finally able to set up his X-ray apparatus on the second floor of the dental practice in Keswick. Since the Southgate house lay empty, the Spareys let it out to an engineer and his family who were badly in need of a home, also lending him, free of charge, the Austin 10 car which he cared for and used over the following six years before it was reunited with Leslie in

Keswick.

Quiet as life appeared to be in the safe haven of the English Lake District, the bombing further south continued unabated, with historic cities such as Bath, Exeter, Canterbury, York, and Coventry being targeted, as well as the endless raids on London and industrial cities. Leslie's sister Elsie, with her husband Wallis and daughters, Eileen and Shirley, were living in the south Lakes industrial town of Barrow-in-Furness when it was bombed during April and May 1941, and during one particularly severe night raid their home was completely destroyed. Thankfully the family were spared, and the following morning they made their way north to Keswick, where they camped for a while with Leslie and Joan in their tiny rented rooms, grateful for a floor and a roof away from the devastation of bombing. As soon as it seemed safe, they returned to Barrow-in-Furness, living in a variety of temporary homes before settling into a disused railway carriage on the beach at Bardsea, overlooking Morecambe Bay. Since the carriage consisted of two separate compartments, living conditions were far from easy, and negotiating their way from one to the other during the blackout became a major operation in itself. Thankfully after a few months a furnished house in nearby Ulverston became available, where they remained until the end of the war.

Although life seemed to be calmer away from the constant bombing further south with Leslie finding a much-needed opportunity for recovering his health, there were still times of extreme stress and worry, especially when he was called to attend an interview for the Royal Army Dental Corps, requiring him to travel to the H.Q. of Western Command at York for his medical examination; however, Leslie needn't have worried, for when the Medical Officer realised the extent of his poor health he was surprised that he had been asked to attend at all, and rejected him with a Grade E rating. On being told the news, Leslie's fellow dentist, Donald Gregg, was greatly relieved, since the dental practice was struggling to cater for the vast number of patients pouring through its door.

Early in 1941 Leslie and Joan joined the Congregational Church, Leslie becoming a Deacon and on occasion taking a mid-week service. In his memoirs he later noted that this period was a major landmark in their spiritual lives and their marriage, not in any way as a consequence of joining the church, but due to a chance interview which they heard on the radio. During the early years of the Second World War there was a good deal of concern in Britain over what were known as the 'Fifth Columnists', the name given to spies and saboteurs who secretly sympathised with the fascists, and who could be anyone from the next-door neighbour to a local shopkeeper; suspicion was rife, and people were strongly encouraged not to engage strangers in conversation. [27] It was in this atmosphere of mistrust that people tried to run their lives as the war continued in earnest, and so it was with great interest that Joan and Leslie heard a very positive voice on the radio one day, declaring that what was needed was a 'Sixth column', people committed to God and to carrying out what they believed to be His plan not only for Britain, but for the world. It was a grand expectation, but in the depths of war with much of the world in the grip of fear as Hitler seemed hell-bent on taking the whole of Europe, the concept of a 'Sixth column' seemed to offer a glimmer of hope. The man who was speaking that day was Jack Winslow, an ordained Anglican priest who for many years had been a missionary for the Church Missionary Society in India, where he had been a pioneer of the Ashram movement, bringing together Christians of many denominations in fellowship with other faiths; he was also connected with Moral Re-Armament.

Leslie and Joan were very impressed and inspired by what they heard on the radio that morning, but how to follow it up didn't appear to be obvious from where they were living in a remote corner of England. The obvious solution seemed to be nothing less than contacting the speaker himself, and so Leslie lost no time in finding out where Jack Winslow lived, and in writing not only to thank him for his ideas, but also inviting him to visit their home in Keswick if he was ever in the vicinity. A prompt response was just the beginning of a friendship which lasted for many years, and as soon as accommodation could be found for him in Keswick, Jack arrived for a brief visit. Not one to miss an opportunity, Leslie arranged for his guest to give a talk on the 'Sixth Column' in Keswick, booking the Congregational Hall and inviting as many local people as possible to attend. Not only did the Catholic, Anglican, and Nonconformist clergy turn up, but so also did the Vicar of St. John's church, of whom it was reported that he would never attend a public meeting where other Christian denominations were involved. The meeting was chaired by Professor Darnley-Naylor, an ex-Liberal politician and Governor of Keswick School, whose wife Leslie had known in London in connection with the League of Nations Union. Jack Winslow was also invited to speak at a Rotary Club lunch, as well as giving sermons in Crosthwaite Church. This burst of activity focusing on spiritual matters during one of the bleakest periods of European history was a catalyst for future events in Keswick over the following years, including a week-long conference on 'Training in Christian Faith and Service', which was organised by Leslie, with Jack Winslow leading the programme.

Leslie and Joan had no doubt that the spiritual path they were following offered answers not only to their own problems, but also to the problems of the world, and as they immersed themselves in the principles and beliefs which Moral Re-Armament promoted, they were laying the foundation for what powered the rest of their lives. What they may not have been aware of at the time was that through their move to Keswick, they were actually living in the town where the Oxford Group, later to be known as Moral Re-Armament, had been born over thirty years earlier.

Despite being a year of new spiritual vistas for Leslie and Joan, 1941 also brought with it great sadness, when on 18th December Leslie's mother died from peritonitis at the age of 72; had antibiotics been available, it's quite probable that she would have survived, but unfortunately the miracle of antibiotics was still some way into the future. Amy's

death was a dreadful blow to the family, most particularly
for Herbert, who found the prospect of living without his
beloved Amy almost too much to bear. Once the funeral was
over the immediate problem was finding suitable accommodation for the whole family, which with all the refugees and
evacuees filling every available room in Keswick, seemed an
almost impossible task. However, luck seemed to be on their
side when they spotted an advertisement in the window
of number 19, Southey Street, which was offering two
bedrooms, lounge, kitchen and shared bathroom; following
an interview with the owner-occupier, a Mr. Dunbobbin,
they were able to move in immediately, thankful for finding
what appeared to be such suitable premises so quickly.
However, several friends lost no time in voicing their deep
concern, since the two previous tenants had suffered terrible
anxiety and mental stress due to living in the same house as
Mr. Dunbobbin; but with no alternative available to them,
the Spareys accepted the challenge and settled into their
new home.

Amy in Keswick shortly before her death. ... Herbert.

The move went smoothly, and everything appeared
to be going well until Joan offered to help Mr. Dunbobbin

with his shopping. Due to severe arthritis he was unable to leave the house, and although Joan was keen to help him, he turned her offer down. However, a day or two later he was seen lowering a basket out of his first-floor window and asking passers-by to do his shopping, having informed them that Mrs. Sparey refused to help him! His behaviour towards his tenants became so unpredictable that the only way they felt safe at night was to wedge their bedroom door shut with a chair. If the situation was already extremely stressful and the atmosphere tense, it was about to get much worse. One day when Mr. Dunbobbin was sharpening a knife in the kitchen he looked menacingly at Leslie, and told him that in the Bible it is written that "the wicked shall be slain"; this was the final straw, and Leslie and Joan immediately began searching for alternative accommodation. Thankfully they didn't have to look for very long, soon finding a flat over the electricity shop in St John's Street. But moving out of Mr. Dunbobbin's house was no simple matter, for rumour had it that going from past experience, he would be extremely angry when he realised that his tenants were moving out; in order to ensure that they left his premises in an impeccable condition, the Spareys arranged for a friend to make an inspection, and although she declared the rooms to be clean and tidy, they nevertheless received a letter from Mr. Dunbobbin, complaining that they had left the rooms in a disgusting state and that he would tell everybody about their unacceptable behaviour. Nothing came of it, needless to say, and a few years later Mr.Dunbobbin passed away with no friends to mourn him.

Chapter Fifteen

Home

At what point Leslie and Joan decided to settle in Keswick for good isn't clear; Leslie's health had improved considerably since moving away from London, and he was happy working with Mr. Gregg in Keswick, despite the ongoing difficulties concerning accommodation. The war continued to be a backdrop to daily life, with the refugees and evacuees no doubt a constant reminder that hostilities were ongoing. A letter which Joan wrote to Leslie for Christmas 1943 gives some insight to their relationship, which had deepened spiritually as a result of their commitment to the principles of Moral-Re-Armament: "I feel that you know me inside out," she wrote, "and I need never worry that you will misunderstand me. It is so wonderful to have such a husband and companion; we are one mind. I am sorry when I am unruly and naughty, but it is just high spirits - I am younger than you and more jumpy."

Living in the small flat above the electricity shop in St John's Street was the final difficulty the Spareys were to endure as far as living space was concerned, for they were delighted when a lovely Georgian house opposite the park on Penrith Road became available, made possible by the generosity of the owner, who was happy for them to live there at a rent they could afford. An added bounty was that since the house was unfurnished they were able to use their own furniture, which until that point had been in storage in a garage in Station Road. At last, after several difficult years of living in temporary accommodation which was either too small or unsuitable, Leslie and Joan were able to create an environment which really felt like home. There was also space for visitors, of which there was a steady stream as the war finally seemed to be coming to an end. Leslie's niece, Shirley, stayed for an extended period while her parents took care of arrangements to move back to London, where Wallis had been appointed as a Conservative agent in Dulwich. Whilst Leslie enjoyed the opportunity of teaching his niece elementary French, Joan made sure that everyday life was enjoyable, no doubt relishing the companionship of someone of her own sex who wasn't far behind her in age. Shirley remembered that spending time with Joan "was such fun. We went to the swing park every afternoon, walked for miles, and larked around with Grandpa Sparey (Herbert), even though he protested! On a deeper note, I received my first, and lasting, love of things spiritual and musical, both of which were in abundance in the lovely house in Penrith Road."

Friends and family weren't the only visitors to the house in Penrith Road. Leslie and Joan also opened their home to people in need, although it's not quite clear how they met or how many there were. At the end of his memoirs Leslie refers to a young Czech girl who was staying with them before the war ended, and who had fled the Nazis having lost all the members of her family. Her fragile mental state made life very difficult for those trying to help her in Keswick. On one occasion she ordered new glasses, and on realising that they improved her sight she became convinced that the answer to all the world's problems was simply a matter of new 'spectacles'; she was very keen to get in touch with Hitler as soon as possible in order to arrange for him to buy new glasses, and thus finish the war! When she eventually travelled to London by train she was admitted to a mental hospital, where she not only became convinced that Leslie and Joan were her parents, but also gave her surname as Sparey. Unfortunately nothing could be done for the poor young woman, and she died a few weeks later.

For whatever reason, Leslie finished recording his memoirs at this point; over the following years he noted significant events in his annual diary, albeit in practically illegible handwriting, and he occasionally typed out various statements which are useful in tying up one or two loose ends. On the occasion of their Golden Wedding many decades later, he reflected on what had been the basis of his happy and successful marriage to Joan; having mentioned their combined interests in music and history, he then wrote, "a living faith is fundamental, and in our case we have based all our decisions, both great and small, on the principle that God has a plan for each one, and the solution to all problems and decisions is to try to discover what is God's way in each case. It's not always easy by any means, and of course we have made many mistakes, but it really is the cure for disagreements. --- We have found that the best way to deal with irritations is to tell each other --- at the right time of course; not at all an easy matter! --- Criticism of any kind must be carried out with great sensitivity and real caring, with the prerequisite that it is I who need to change first. None of us likes being criticised --- I hate it! --- Honesty between us is essentially the basis of our relationship, which should be a partnership." He also pointed out the importance of being a good and patient listener. Later on in the statement he touched on the subject of children, and in reference to the end of the war he wrote, "due to the five war years and threatened invasion it seemed right to postpone the issue, but we were grateful to a wise friend who in 1945 reminded us about what we were missing." Apparently they lost no time in taking this advice seriously, for sometime in March 1946, Joan was able to tell him that she was going to have a baby.

35, Station Road, Keswick. The house in which Leslie and Joan eventually settled, and where Leslie had his dental practice. The photo was taken several years later, with Joan making her presence known from one of the windows.

By this time the Spareys had made the decision to stay in Keswick. There's no record of what happened to the family home in Dunsmure Road, although it's safe to assume that compensation would have been paid by the War Damage Commission before the house was repaired and sold. It's probable that the house in Southgate was also sold, along with the Ibach piano, which certainly never made it to Keswick.

By the end of 1945 Mr. Gregg had announced that he was ready to retire from dentistry, and having made the decision to take over the practice Leslie and Joan had begun preparing to move into number 35, Station Road, which was to be their home for the next forty years. Leslie's diary for January 1946 mentions several visits to number 35, with "view curtains", "see Gregg re instruments", and "we take measurements at 35", all paving the way for their big move. By this time the Austin 10 had been in London for six years, and finally, on March 14th the Spareys took the train south in order to drive the car to Keswick in time for their move on April 9th. Forever meticulous in his calculations and forward planning, Leslie noted in the back of his diary that the Austin had clocked up 44,000 miles when he collected it, and 44,404 when they arrived in Keswick; it was now twelve years old, and still had several years of life left in it.

Leslie's 1946 diary gives plenty of information, most of it concerned with taking over the dental practice, moving into their new home, and Joan's pregnancy, which involved monthly retreats to bed for a week and frequent visits to a doctor in Carlisle. A previous miscarriage had obviously made the hopeful parents-to-be rather nervous, but they needn't have worried, because the baby arrived on December 28th, albeit a week later than expected. [28]

Carolyn's arrival didn't in any way prevent Leslie and Joan from making positive plans in relation to the other two most important areas of their life together, the work of Moral Re-Armament and music. As far as the first was concerned, regular meetings were held both in Keswick and in nearby Grasmere, where the artist William Heaton Cooper and his wife, the sculptress Ophelia Gordon Bell, were also adherents. As far as music was concerned, in January 1947 Leslie bought himself a radiogram, [29] and at some point Joan took possession of a beautiful second-hand Bechstein grand piano which came from a retired piano professor at the Royal Academy of Music in London; this opened up the possibility of playing chamber music with other amateur musicians in the town, and as the year progressed chamber music became a regular feature in the diary.

Opportunities for hearing music were few and far between in Keswick at that time, apart from occasional concerts given by visiting artists and private gatherings for the purpose of listening to gramophone records. Leslie and Joan had been spoilt for choice when they lived in London, and probably missed the wonderful live performances they had taken for granted at the time. Thus it was that a tiny seed was sown, probably no more than a passing thought at first, but one which Leslie felt compelled to pursue, for on September 30th he arranged a meeting with local music teacher Leslie Hindley in order to discuss the possibility of forming a Music Club. This was followed by a second meeting a week later, with Joan attending, and by October 24th such was the enthusiasm from other music lovers in the town that a committee was set up with Leslie appointed as chairman and Mr. Hindley as secretary; it's thanks to his meticulous minute-keeping that the initial history of the Keswick Music Club, (now Society) is still available. (See *Appendix 3*)

Within two months the newly functioning Music Club was able to hold its very first public concert, which took place on December 3rd. The artists were violinist, Nona Liddell, and pianist Daphne Ibbott, who had been a close friend of Joan's when as children they both studied the piano with Miss Floyd in London. Nona and Daphne stayed with the Spareys, rehearsing in the elegant first floor lounge looking out over the park. The story has been told many times, that as the rehearsal was taking place, Carolyn, now 11 months old, was intent on disrupting the music by screaming heartily from her playpen; and that Nona said to Joan, "Carolyn is either completely tone deaf, or extremely musical". As it turned out, the second option proved to be prophetic ---

--- but that's another story.

Leslie and Joan.

Appendix I

The League of Nations

The League of Nations Union (LNU) was created in Britain in October 1918 in order to support the concept of international justice and collective security, and was essentially the merger of two existing organisations, the League of Free Nations Association and the League of Nations Society, both of which had focused on ways to bring about world peace, particularly through disarmament. Based on the principles of the League of Nations, the LNU's remit was to gain permanent peace between nations. Lord Robert Cecil (see below) was president of the British LNU from 1923 to 1945. At the head of the LNU was the General Council which met annually, with the Executive Committee meeting every two weeks and being responsible for campaigns and educational programmes, as well as taking care of reports which came in from LNU branches.

With regard to the formation of the League of Nations, the horrors of World War One had ignited a renewed resolve world-wide to finding a solution for the prevention of wars in the future. A number of political leaders on both sides of the Atlantic believed that there was a desperate need for an organisation which would enable international cooperation and security, and among them were Lord Robert Cecil in Britain and President Woodrow Wilson in the United States. Woodrow Wilson spoke publicly on the matter in May 1916, instructing his chief advisor on

European affairs, Edward House, to put together a plan based on his ideals. Already as the war began there had been a scheme supported by both Britain and the United States, with the British politician, Lowes Dickinson, coining the phrase 'League of Nations' as early as 1914 and outlining a proposal for its organisation.

In Britain Lord Cecil sent out a directive during September 1916, with recommendations for avoiding future wars, and he firmly believed that this document was the catalyst for British support for the League of Nations. As one of the two main architects of the League, (the other being Jan Smuts, Commonwealth statesman), Lord Cecil's focus was on administration and the organisation of meetings. At the Paris Peace Conference in 1919 Cecil and Smuts along with Woodrow Wilson, presented their proposed plans, and after consultation and some compromise, agreement was reached on 25th January for the creation of the League of Nations. However, it wasn't plain sailing, and although Woodrow Wilson was awarded the Nobel Peace prize during that year for his input and his efforts to secure its success, he wasn't able to gain support from the Senate with the result that the United States didn't join.

The League's remit was that it would consist of a General Assembly (representing all member states), an Executive Council (with membership limited to major powers), and a permanent secretariat. All states were required to submit complaints for mediation or judicial inquiry before going to war. Between 28 September 1934 and 23 February 1935, the League had 58 member states, although from then onwards it was clear that the signatories to the League were not prepared to put the principle of collective security into action. As the League failed in its attempts to secure collective security, so more and more people lost faith in it. Germany and Japan withdrew in 1933 and Italy in 1937, followed by the expulsion of the Soviet Union in 1939.

The LNU, however, did make waves in Britain during the period between the two world wars, and was instrumental in positively influencing the opinion of mainstream British society in regard to the remit of the League of Nations, most notably through the churches and national newspapers. The LNU's organisation of the unofficial 1935 Peace Ballot concerning international disarmament and collective security gained over eleven million votes in Britain, its success influencing many politicians at the time, and the positive result publicised throughout the world.

But all attempts to make peace a reality ultimately failed. The League of Nations hadn't been able to prevent the worsening situation in Europe as another war loomed on the horizon, and although it did still exist legally, and although Lord Cecil had received the Nobel Peace Prize in 1937, the League's headquarters at the Palace of Nations in Geneva lay empty for six years until the end of the Second World War. It was in 1943, at the Tehran Conference, that the Allied powers decided to replace the League of Nations with a new body, the United Nations. The final meeting of the League of Nations took place in Geneva in April 1946. Lord Cecil was 81 as he addressed the last session, telling those gathered there that aggression of any kind is an "international crime"; he also stressed that the work for peace depends not solely on the "narrow interests of our own nations, but even more on those great principles of right and wrong which nations, like individuals, depend." He finished by declaring, "the League is dead. Long live the United Nations."

Thus it was that the United Nations superseded the failed League of Nations, and in 1948 the United Nations Association was created in order to support the newly formed United Nations, taking over the management and membership of the LNU and in effect, replacing it.

Appendix 2

A brief overview of Moral Re-Armament

In 1908 an American Christian by the name of Frank Buchman had attended the annual Keswick Convention, a Christian gathering which had begun in 1875 as a focal point for the Higher Life movement in the United Kingdom. It was during a service at the Tithebarn Street Primitive Methodist chapel that Frank Buchman experienced personal spiritual renewal, freeing him from bitterness which had been affecting his life. His transformation and his decision to help change the world by changing himself were just the start of what became a world-wide movement bringing change into many individual and collective lives. The Oxford Group came into being as a result of this spiritual transformation, and changed its name to Moral Re-Armament in 1938. (see Chapter 13)

Most people in Britain who became involved in Moral Re-Armament during the Second World War came from a Christian background; due to the fine principles it stood for, reflecting the feelings of many concerned people at the time, it gained wide support from public figures in Britain. In 1940 the famous novelist, Daphne du Maurier, wrote a book which told the stories of people in Britain whose lives had been radically changed through the movement. The title of the book was Come Wind, Come Weather, selling six hundred and fifty thousand copies in Britain alone, and dedicated to Frank Buchman, the founder of Moral Re-Armament. The British tennis champion, H.W. Austin, who in 1931 had been ranked as the World no. 2, edited the book, Moral Rearmament (The Battle for Peace), which in turn sold half a million copies. Over the following decades the movement gained an army of adherents who lived and worked in many different parts of the world, and who came from various faith and cultural backgrounds

Moral Re-Armament's tenet was basically to make possible reconciliation between opposing factions, whether they were two people, two groups, or two countries. After the Second World War MRA was extremely active, both in Britain, where during industrial disputes it worked to bring together white collar and shop floor workers in an attempt to forge a solution, and further afield, most notably in Africa and Asia as countries moved towards independence from colonial rule. The most notable instance of reconciliation at the time was that of France and Germany immediately after the war; it involved a French woman by the name of Irène Laure who had been a member of the French Resistance and an MP during the 1945 parliament, and whose family had suffered under German occupation. Keen to be a part of the reconstruction of Europe following the war she accepted an invitation to attend a conference at the MRA centre in Caux, above Lake Geneva. However, when a group of Germans arrived she was so angry that she decided to leave immediately. As a result of Frank Buchman's question asking how she expected Europe to be rebuilt without the Germans, she took refuge in her room and battled with her conscience until finally she felt able to face meeting a German woman, with whom she then shared all her hatred and resentment. The German was a Clarita von Trott, whose husband Adam had been executed following the failed attempt on Hitler's life, and whose children had been put in an SS-run orphanage while their mother was in prison. When Clarita apologised to Irène for failing to resist hard enough, and for the suffering this had caused, Irène felt freed from her own hatred and bitterness, and asked to speak in the main meeting in Caux, which included 100 Germans amongst the 500 gathered. Having talked about her involvement in the French Resistance, she explained that although nothing could be forgotten she could make the decision to forgive, after which she completely stunned the audience by asking for forgiveness for her hatred. This was the beginning of what became her mission as she travelled through Germany with her message of forgiveness, addressing political meetings, speaking on the radio, and reaching thousands; much later, in 1958, the German Chancellor, Adenhauer, was to state that Irène and her husband Victor had contributed more than anything else to reconciliation between France and Germany.

In 2001 Moral Re-Armament changed its name to Initiatives of Change.

Appendix 3

The Music Society: a legacy for Keswick

On February 12th 1947, the pianist Louis Kentner, (who amongst other achievements had been heard in Richard Addinsell's Warsaw Concerto from the soundtrack of the 1941 film, Dangerous Moonlight) gave a piano recital at the Rawnsley Hall in Keswick, one of the rare occasions at the time that the townspeople had access to world-class live performances. This was maybe one of the seeds which led to Leslie's decision to discuss the possibility of forming a Music Club with music teacher Leslie Hindley on September 30th. Mr. Hindley was a lovable eccentric who named his car Thelma, fed it ice cream, and congratulated it when it managed to climb a steep hill. He also collected pieces of broken glass wherever he went, keeping it in an attache case in order to protect both people and animals from injuring themselves, and he delighted in announcing how much he had collected at the end of each week! Through his passion for fireworks the Fireworks Committee donated over £30 towards a commemoration of his service to the Music Club, which decided to buy a first class piano stool.

Thankfully detailed minute-keeping offers a window on how events proceeded. On Wednesday October 15th 1947 about fifty-five interested people gathered at the Masonic Hall, St. John's Street, where they unanimously agreed with chairman Leslie Sparey's suggestion that a club should be formed. The resolution stated that "this meeting, believing that it would be good to bring together all those who are interested in music whether as performers or listeners, and that every encouragement should be given to the development of music --- proposes the formation of a society to be known as the Keswick Music Club. Its main objectives would be to stimulate the latent musical interest of the district, and to bring people together for the purpose of ensemble playing or singing; informal meeting or discussion circle; the organisation of concerts both private and public, from time to time; and the arranging of gramophone recitals and lectures." [30]

The first committee meeting took place at 35, Station Road, on October 24th, when the officers were elected as follows: chairman, Leslie Sparey; treasurer, R. Mustchin (violin teacher); and secretary, Leslie Hindley. Julius Katay, (see chapter 14), who by all accounts had set up a small orchestra in Keswick shortly after the war, was present, as were Lady Rochdale and a handful of others. At this meeting the chairman agreed to contact the Art's Council in order to apply for funding, Mr. Mustchin took on responsibility for organising ensemble playing, Lady Rochdale offered her beautiful home, Lingholm, for gramophone evenings, and Mr. Hindley agreed to look into the matter of professional concerts, with the help of six others who aren't named. Mr. Mustchin was authorised to sign cheques.

Subsequent committee meetings were held on November 12th and 29th, and within just a couple of months of the idea being muted, the Keswick Music Club was a going concern, although Lord Rochdale had regretfully declined the offer of becoming president. There was a recommendation that three professional concerts should be held during the initial six months with tickets selling at three shillings and sixpence and two shillings, season tickets for seven shillings and sixpence, and with the season's programme to be printed on membership cards. The efficient committee dealt ably with matters of finance, setting up a constitution and securing the Rawnsley Hall at Keswick School for the professional concerts, with club concerts and socials taking place at the Keswick Hotel. These club concerts were to be given by local groups including The Mountain Singers, the Keswick Ladies' Choir, and Whitehaven and Workington Orchestral Societies. Negotiations were in hand for exemption from Entertainment Duty, twelve pounds had been paid as a deposit for the first concert, and The Arts's Council of Great Britain had agreed to meet all artists' fees for the coming season.

The first professional concert was to take place on December 3rd at the Rawnsley Hall, (Nona Liddell and Daphne Ibbott, see chapter 15). The secretary noted that "these charming artists played sonatas by Beethoven and Dohnanyi and each a group of solos. There was a more than satisfactory attendance and all noted the evening as being a splendid send off." On December 15th a party travelled by coach to Whitehaven to attend a concert given by the BBC Northern Orchestra conducted by Charles Groves, and the first gramophone recital took place at the Keswick Hotel on December 17th, fifty five members present, and with Leslie as one of the facilitators. According to the minutes Mr.

Grocock added to the enjoyment "by his skilful handling of the amplification", whilst a decision was taken that the lights should be lowered in future, and that the members should "tactfully" be requested not to smoke. It was also agreed that a "gratuity of five shillings" should be given to the hotel porter. The club social on January 10th, 1948 consisted of a variety of performances given by club members, with "20 questions as an interlude." By this time the club had one hundred and ninety-eight members, and the tidy sum of £70 in the bank.

The diary was awash with concerts and social events from this point onwards. Of particular interest was Professor Katay's Keswick Ladies' Choir, which performed in February 1948, the secretary commenting that it "was again realised how fortunate Keswick is to have a choir so ably trained, for they once again gave of their very best. Mr. Katay gave some pianoforte solos with conspicuous success ---".

And so it continued, year on year, the Music Club providing the town with a wonderful choice of music given by visiting professionals, local amateurs, as well as evenings of recorded music. Some of Britain's most famous and much-loved celebrities performed in the first few years, names such as The Boyd Neil Orchestra, Joyce Grenfell, Carl Dolmetch, Leon Goossens and John Ogdon; the list goes on. The minute-taking and meticulous recording of each and every event stopped at the end of May, 1951, but the club went from strength to strength, and is still functioning successfully, with concerts now taking place in the beautiful Theatre by the Lake.

Notes

Passages in double inverted commas are taken from original diaries and memoirs, with the exception of the quote taken from the Daily Express (pages 96/97).

[1] A back kitchen used for washing dishes and laundry.

[2] Information taken from The Conquest of Epidemic Disease: A Chapter in the History of Ideas. Charles-Edward Amory Winslow. Page 370.

[3] For anyone reading this history who has a family interest, or is simply curious, the family connection is a follows: Amy's sister Lizzie, who had married Ferguson Nutt Epps, had a daughter by the name of Florence (Florrie), who in turn married Morgan Kelly. At the time during which they lived with Leslie and his family, Morgan and Florrie already had two sons, Adrian, who was two and a half, and Reginald (Reggie), at just a few months. Reginald became a very successful neurologist in adult life, most notably as consultant neurologist at St. Thomas's Hospital and the National Hospital for Neurology and Neurosurgery, London. He married Peggy Stone, and they had four children, the second of whom became Sir Christopher William Kelly, who held various positions including Chairman of the NSPCC, Chairman of the Financial Obudsman Service, and Chairman of the Committee on Standards in Public Life. Adrian married Monica Edwards, and the second of their four children became Baroness Hollins, professor of psychiatry of learning disability at St George's, University of London,

also for a time Chairman of the British Medical Association, and a member of the House of Lords. This is a very minimal account of only a handful of Leslie's immediate relatives, all of them deserving of mention but space being limited.

[4] Books by B.C. Boulter include Rome Illustrated. Parish Plays no. 26 The Mystery of Epiphany. Simon de Montfort, Champion of Christian Liberty.

[5] Originally set up by the university in 1857 in order to improve middle-class education and be of benefit to people not in a financial position to offer university education for their children.

[6] 2LO was the second radio station to regularly broadcast in the United Kingdom (the first was 2MT). It began broadcasting on 11 May 1922, for one hour a day from the seventh floor of Marconi House in London's Strand.

[7] An interesting connection is that Leslie's daughter, who is the author of this biography, performed in the first London production of Jesus Christ Superstar at the Palace Theatre in August 1972. She also took part in the 1972 recording. (vinyl and tape. MGA records - MDKS 8008)

[8] Run by the students, University Rag societies are charitable fundraising organisations, and are found in many British universities.

[9] The play was set in a run-down boarding house, the residents

grappling with a variety of personal, relationship, and social problems. A mysterious stranger arrives on the scene and encourages everyone to address their differences as well as pursuing their dreams of a better life; this stranger was in effect suggestive of a Christ-like figure.

[10] Decimalisation was introduced in Britain in 1971. Money was made up of £ (pounds), s (shillings) and p (pence), with 20 shillings per pound and 12 pence per shilling.

[11] John Hampden (ca. 1595 - 1643) English politician and one of the leading parliamentarians involved in challenging the authority of Charles I of England prior to the English Civil War. He became a national figure when he stood trial in 1637 for his refusal to be taxed for ship money, and was one of the Five Members whose attempted unconstitutional arrest by King Charles I in the House of Commons of England in 1642 sparked the Civil War. In 1643 he died of wounds received on Chalgrove Field during the war, becoming a celebrated English patriot.

[12] They lived for a while in Packington Street, Islington with two lodgers, widows of 74 and 78 respectively. In 1891 they were living in Broughton Road, Stoke Newington, with their first five children, and ten years later they had moved once again, to Chisholm Road, eight children in tow, the eldest 19, and the youngest no more than a baby. By 1911 they were all at 35, Maury Road, Stoke Newington, all six of the children old enough to be married still single and employed, with the last two still at school.

[13] Someone who has completed an apprenticeship in a trade, is fully competent, but hasn't gone through the necessary steps in order to become a master of that trade.

[14] In the possession of the author.

[15] 53 - 156, Lower Clapton Road Hackney. First established in 1889 by the Salvation Army, at a time when maternity hospitals only accepted married women; the home was for poor young women, many pregnant and unmarried, a condition which was not accepted in general society. All the Sisters, and the Matron, were officers in the Salvation Army.

[16] Board schools were the first state run schools.

[17] Sir Charles Barnard Groves CBE, 10 March 1915 - 20 June 1992, was awarded many honours for his service to music, including Officer of the Order of the British Empire (OBE) in 1958, a Commander of the Order (CBE) in 1968, and a knighthood in 1973. He became a freeman of the City of London in 1976, was elected an honorary member of the Royal Philharmonic Society in 1990, and received doctorates from four universities. He was the first conductor to direct a complete cycle of Gustav Mahler's symphonies in Britain, and during the 1970s he regularly conducted the Last Night of the Proms in the Albert Hall. Of personal interest to me, the author, is that during the 1980s when I was principal viola with the BBC Scottish Symphony Orchestra, I worked with Sir Charles regularly; every time we met he asked, "and how is Joan?".

[18] Solomon Cutner was born in the East End of London in 1902, and became a world-famous solo pianist, known simply as Solomon. He was known particularly for his almost legendary interpretation of Beethoven, broadcasting all thirty-two piano sonatas for the BBC.

[19] Bearing in mind that the concert didn't start until 8pm, the audience no doubt required a great deal of stamina to see it through to the end, not to mention the hard-worked BBC Symphony Orchestra and their conductor, Henry Wood.

[20] The programme consisted of:

- Roman Carnival Overture of Berlioz.
- Andante from Mozart's Cassation in G, (Cassation is a genre akin to the Serenade and Divertimento) K63
- The finale of Orchestral Suite 'No. 6'; orchestral arrangement of Bach's E major Partita for solo violin by Henry Wood.
- Rachmaninov's Piano Concerto No. 2 in C minor, soloist, Solomon.
- Aria from Weber's opera,Oberon, 'Ocean, thou mighty monster', sung by Eva Turner.
- Symphony No. 5, Beethoven.
- 'Brigg Fair', Delius.
- Puccini, Aria 'In questa reggia' fromTurandot, soloist Eva Turner.
- Ravel, Boléro (http://www.bbc.co.uk/events/e2pfx)

[21] Cecil had been one of the architects of the League of Nations,

was a committed supporter and defender of it, and was awarded the Nobel Peace Prize in 1937. For a short review of the League of Nations see Appendix 1.

[22] By the time Eva was arrested in 1937, OGPU had actually become the NKVD, although from the newspaper accounts at the time, they were still being referred to as OGPU. OGPU was the acronym for the secret police of the Soviet Union from 1922 to 1934, and also the principal secret police agency which dealt with finding, arresting, and liquidating people who were considered to be anarchists, as well as other dissident left-wing factions in the early Soviet Union. In 1934, OGPU became the NKVD (People's Commissariat For Internal Affairs), and in 1946, the KGB.

[23] An item of furniture; a tabletop set on a base, or chest, able to pivot into a vertical position when the table wasn't being used, forming the back of a seat, or bench.

[24] Buchman, Frank N.D., Remaking the World (London, 1955), p. 46.

[25] Unser Kampf was published as the Second World War was beginning, the author attempting to offer a solution to the problems facing the world by promoting the adoption of a system of common ownership, the introduction of an international force using Esperanto as its language, and advocating the concept of a new world order under the leadership of men who were passionate to see it happen. The struggle referred to was that of making the dream a reality.

[26] 'Keswick and the Lake District', The Manchester Guardian, 24 March 1934, p. 17.

[27] The term had been coined by Emilio Mola Vidal, a Nationalist general during the Spanish Civil War, who, in an effort to take the capital, Madrid, had described his supporters within the city as a 'fifth column' reinforcing his four military columns.

[28] The baby was the author, Carolyn Sparey Fox.

[29] An item of furniture combining both radio and record player.

[30] From the first page of the original 'Minutes of Keswick Music Club', written by hand. At present in the possession of the author. All the quotes in this Appendix from the same source.